THE POWER OF INFLUENCE: CULTIVATING CATALYSTS, UNVEILING THE FORCES BEHIND TRANSFORMATIONAL LEADERSHIP

By: Mustafa Nejem

Table of Contents

Chapter 1

INTRODUCTION AND OVERVIEW:
THE POWER OF INFLUENCE IN RANSFORMATIONAL LEADERSHIP

The purpose and objectives of this book:

This book was specifically created for people who want to become great leaders but don't know how to start. It aims at helping readers unlock their personal leadership potentials thereby inspiring change within their organizations and communities.

This book seeks to define the importance of influence in leadership towards sustainable change. It goes beyond transactional approaches and emphasizes transformational leadership as a way of inspiring followers to achieve their full potential.

Furthermore, the purpose of this book is to provide an understanding of the core principles and characteristics of transformational leadership. Some of these terms include catalysts, innovation, collaboration and personal influence which will be defined later. Through practical strategies, real life examples from experts; readers will gain knowledge on what it takes to become such a leader themselves and excel in the workplace, the community and in life.

Readers will find out how they can tell stories that engage others deeply, while at the same time learning how to overcome challenges faced by organizations like theirs when implementing transformative approaches into daily operations. We also provide insight into different theories or models that have informed our thinking about what constitutes good transformational leaders.

Understanding the importance of influence in leadership requires defining the concept. In this book, influence refers to how a leader can motivate and inspire others to achieve exceptional results. This power makes change possible by electrifying individuals and teams towards greatness.

Influential leaders are different because they have an extraordinary ability to make a deep impact on others. They instill a sense of purpose and passion in those around them through their words, actions, and unfailing belief. These leaders know that it is not about forcing people into submission or manipulating them; instead, they encourage others voluntarily accept new ideas while taking control over self-development.

Transformational leadership is all about that. Transactional approaches only consider rewards and punishments when motivating people but transformational leaders go further than that. They inspire their followers so as to enable them to fully utilize what they have got from within themselves. By fostering an environment where growth is encouraged and forging a common vision, these leaders bring out the best in individuals as well as groups.

This book aims at explaining how transformational leadership works in the context of influential leaders using their power of influence for sustainable changes. It seeks answers regarding the driving forces behind transformative abilities as well as uncovering secrets behind these catalysts of change..

Throughout subsequent chapters readers will be taken through captivating real life examples, expert analysis and practical strategies. Each chapter will touch on different aspects related to transformational leadership ranging from understanding catalysts behind change and exploring their characteristics up-to creating innovation within organizations through collaboration among others. Various theories plus models used to explain transformational leadership shall also be discussed within this book.

By the end of this book, readers should gain insight on how to develop personal influence, overcome challenges and create positive impacts in their organizations as well as communities at large. They will also understand different aspects of leadership styles including charismatic, servant based, and transactional amongst others.

The main objective of this book is therefore to motivate and enable future leaders with the necessary tools for realizing their full potential. Whether one is leading a team, managing an organization or trying to make a difference in society, there is much guidance here for readers seeking to cultivate catalysts within themselves or others that can inspire meaningful change.

A transformational leader's influence is very great. This style of leadership sets the stage for understanding the powerful impact influence has on organizations and communities. Unlike transactional approaches that focus on exchanges and rewards, transformational leadership inspires and empowers followers.

Transformational leaders are able to transcend traditional barriers and limitations through their inspirational leadership style. They challenge the status quo, encourage creativity and risk-taking, and inspire others to think big and dream even bigger. By instilling a belief that success is possible and creating a shared sense of purpose, these leaders unlock hidden potential within individuals as well as teams driving extraordinary results.

In addition, transformational leaders place emphasis on the personal growth and development of their followers. They invest in building strong relationships based on trust, respect and empathy. Through their typical use of an authentic leadership approach, they serve as role models and mentors; guiding their followers towards continuous improvement whilst helping them overcome obstacles along the way.

We explore the importance of transformational leadership for readers to understand what sets transformative leaders apart from others in more depth. This includes discovering how inspiration, motivation and empowerment can drive lasting change throughout the text. Throughout this book readers will be able to explore different techniques or strategies used for developing these qualities within themselves as well as others.

Further chapters will examine characteristics of transformational leaders; how catalysts foster innovation & collaboration; leading through challenges & adversity and challenges faced by such leaders etc. We shall study various theories including: charismatic leadership theory; servant leadership theory; transactional leadership theory; and finally authentic leadership theory together so that we can get an overall view about the role and power of transformational leadership in action.

Readers will not only gain knowledge about transformational leadership but also have practical tools and strategies that will help them develop catalysts within themselves or other people and by the end of this book with this information at hand they can now embark on a journey where they become effective agents for changing lives around them through impactful leadership within their organizations as well as the communities beyond it. This section also gives a background understanding of transformational leadership and forms part one of our introduction which lays down foundations for understanding core principles defining this powerful style of leadership, setting the groundwork and the main principles, terms and concepts which will be discussed in more detail in subsequent chapters.

What is a transformational leader and what does transformational leadership mean:

Transformational leaders differ from transactional ones by inspiring followers towards reaching their fullest potential instead of just exchanging rewards for performance. Influential leaders can create lasting changes within organizations and communities through such action. It should be emphasized that leadership is about the power of influence and those who have it can easily motivate or inspire others to achieve extraordinary results.

To gain an insight into what readers should expect to learn throughout this book, we will provide an overview of key chapters and sections. This creates anticipation as well as setting clear expectations for the rest of the content laying the groundwork for an open and receptive mind. Learning is about building from solid foundations after-all.

Be prepared, unlocking your full leadership potential and cultivating change within yourself as well as among others, will lead you on a journey to becoming effective agents for meaningful change and this will have many effects, affecting your life, both business and personal.

Transformational leadership is fundamentally a concept that aims to explain how effective leaders can bring about positive change in their organizations. This book is divided into multiple in-depth chapters, each of which offers valuable insights and practical guidance for aspiring leaders who want to be transformational in their style of leadership.

What are catalysts in relation to transformational leadership?

Catalysts are crucial elements within the realms of transformational leadership as they drive positive change and inspire greatness in individuals as well as organizations (bass & riggio 2006). So what exactly is a catalyst? In simple terms, a catalyst refers to any dynamic element that ignites transformation while pushing others towards realizing their true potentials.

There are specific qualities and behaviors which differentiate catalysts from other people. They possess intense sense of purpose and passion that keeps them moving forward in order to leave a mark behind. Additionally, there is an infectious enthusiasm with which they approach work thereby creating motivation among those nearby for collective action towards changing things for the better.

Furthermore, such persons display unwavering determination when it comes to overcoming obstacles or developing new alternatives. They do not allow setbacks or failures hinder them but instead see them as opportunities through which one can learn something new about themselves or improve upon what they already know (Kaufman et al., 2015). Besides, these individuals easily embrace changes occurring around them hence inspiring others also to do likewise whenever necessary in their own lives.

Catalysts are important in that they motivate other people towards achieving transformative goals. They establish a shared purpose and direction through their visionary mindset and charismatic presence. Such leaders communicate visions which resonate with the hearts as well as minds of followers thereby creating belief among them on how together they can effect change.

Moreover, catalysts encourage innovation, creativity and thinking beyond boundaries within an organization or group (Kaufman et al., 2015). They promote diverse perspectives, challenge existing norms and provide room for trying new things including taking risks. By facilitating creative thinking while encouraging calculated risks among team members, catalysts usually unlock hidden potentials leading to breakthrough solutions.

Transformational leadership cannot exist without catalysts who act as the driving force behind it (Kaufman et al., 2015). These individuals encompass qualities needed when one wants to inspire greatness in others or even because certain changes happen. Therefore, any aspiring leader should acknowledge the presence of such powers which make up the favorable environment, an environment for change characterized by innovation, collaboration and meaningful and lasting transformation.

Unpacking catalysts: the power to ignite change:

This section explores further on what distinguishes people as catalysts for change at their core. There are unique attributes that differentiate catalysts enabling them to ignite transformation while inspiring greatness in others too.

Catalysts are defined by their unwavering passion. This is due to their most elemental belief that change is possible. The passion serves as a fuel for action and is infectious to others.

The work of catalysts also involves being flexible and resilient when faced with difficulties. They welcome any form of change and see it as an opportunity for growth. Instead of giving up on something because it didn't go according to plan, they use it for future innovation or improvement. Their adaptability during times of uncertainty gives others confidence to break through limits and look beyond what they already know.

Another quality demonstrated by catalysts is excellent communication skills. They can easily express what they want done in regards to their idea thereby motivating other people who listen to them speak or write down their thoughts about things related directly or indirectly with their vision. Being able to effectively communicate about objectives and hopes create a shared sense of purpose among team members while driving everyone towards achieving transformative goals.

There are several other traits exhibited by catalysts such as empathy as well as emotional intelligence. These natural leaders possess a deep understanding of those being led by them plus they genuinely concern themselves about the welfare and success thereof. As a result, trust, loyalty and commitment arise since these persons are made to feel special within a supportive environment whereby their opinions count thus leading into the inevitable creation of an atmosphere where everyone feels valued, an innovation inspiring environment that nearly always results in dramatic increases in efficiency and productivity as well as employee retention.

Moreover, good leaders lead through example which means that whatever one does must be seen in others for effective guidance purposes especially in organizations where there are many employees working together toward achieving common goals. By acting this way, people will believe them more than if they had just said something without showing any signs of doing so first.

In conclusion, catalysts possess some qualities which are not found in other leaders thus making them unique individuals who deserve recognition whenever leadership issues come up for discussion purposes either at work (promotion) the community (elections), or just by getting more out of life in general. It is therefore clear enough that one cannot become a catalyst by merely showing up at some event but rather it requires personal effort combined with an unquenchable thirst for success together with proper guidance from experienced mentors so as to achieve your desired outcomes within the shortest period possible.

As a whole, catalyst behaviors are more than the typical qualities of an 'average' leader. They have an inborn ability to cause change and inspire people to be great, leading to working together towards attaining transformational objectives for teams. Through recognizing these fundamental characteristics, individuals may develop such traits in themselves as well as others thereby creating a lasting impact on society.

Chapter 2

UNDERSTANDING CATALYSTS:
IGNITING CHANGE AND INSPIRING GREATNESS
*****

In this chapter, we will look deeper into the 'catalysts' concept and how they influence innovation and creativity in organizations. We are going to discuss how catalysts create the environment that promotes innovative thinking, creative problem solving as well as out-of-box approaches to challenges.

As discussed in the context of transformational leadership, a catalyst is an active force for change and inspiration for greatness. These people have special characteristics enabling them to motivate others towards achieving transformative goals. They can see possibilities where others see obstacles while having a natural ability to ignite enthusiasm and passion in those around them.

A catalyst's ability to foster innovation and creativity is one of their key roles. Catalysts appreciate the need for individuals to think outside the box, explore new ideas and take risks. They nurture an experimental culture that welcomes failure as a chance for growth and learning.

Through their leadership, catalysts establish a safe and supportive environment where team members feel empowered to share their thoughts openly with others on the team. This creates psychological safety which allows for collaboration and cross-pollination of ideas. Catalysts create trustful relationships where diverse perspectives are recognized as valuable.

To show how innovation is driven by catalysts; we give examples of real-life leaders who used these agents of change within their companies or institutions. Such leaders have built cultures that embrace innovation beyond limits. Their stories inspire us and teach us how teams can be both creative and successful by fully utilizing such catalysts for change.

By understanding the role played by catalysts in driving innovation as well as creativity; aspiring transformational leaders can also learn some important lessons about creating innovative thinking environments where problems are solved differently from what might be expected. Throughout this chapter winning strategies employed by successful catalysts are highlighted including how they encourage innovative behaviors among employees and promote collaboration among diverse groups in order to facilitate breakthrough ideas creation.

With these strategies' leaders can turn their organizations into centers of innovation where fresh thoughts prevail and transformational change becomes normal. By recognizing the power that catalysts possess, leaders can unlock their team's true potential thereby leading to greatness within themselves and others.

One of many such examples includes Jane Thompson who was a CEO at a technology company which had been struggling with innovation and adaptation issues due its rapidly changing markets. She realized that her firm needed a complete overhaul hence she embarked on redefining her company's vision and culture; this was achieved through various initiatives like designating time for innovations, forming cross departmental teams besides rewarding employees with creative suggestions all things aimed at promoting creativity collaboration. Thompson became an agent of transformation within her organization by creating an atmosphere that encouraged risk taking experimentation; her visionary leadership coupled with indomitable spirit motivated employees to embrace changes resulting into pioneering products, increased market share and sales volume.

Michael Rodriguez, the principal of a struggling urban high school, is another remarkable leader who acted as a catalyst for change. Rodriguez was faced with huge challenges such as low graduation rates and a disengaged student body. However, he did not embrace mediocrity but rather transformed the school into an academic excellence hub. Personalized learning strategies, increased student support services and partnerships with local businesses were some of the things that Rodriguez implemented as part of his comprehensive plan. Through his unwavering commitment and great communication skills, he motivated both his staff and students to believe in themselves and work hard towards achieving their goals. Under his watch, the school witnessed a significant rise in graduation rates as well as academic achievements.

Through these illustrations, we can see how visionaries can use their actions and tactics to light up transformation within their associations or communities. Leaders like these show that catalysts go beyond simply pointing out problems – they actively seek solutions while motivating others to do likewise. These transformational leaders have shown resilience, passion and adaptability which enable others to realize their full potential within their respective environment.

We will discover more about power of catalysts in bringing about positive changes when we delve into the stories behind some more well-known influential leaders later in the book. Their experiences serve as lessons for those who want to be transformational leaders since they give an insight on what qualities are necessary for one to become a catalyst just like them.to know how they did it and what we can learn from those strategies can help us in our own journey towards transformational leadership and becoming a catalyst for change.

Practical techniques for developing catalyst qualities within oneself and others will be discussed in the next section of this chapter. Knowing how to build traits such as passion, adaptability and resilience will foster a culture of transformational leadership where people are motivated by greatness around them. It is important to note that while some individuals possess innate catalyst traits, such as passion, adaptability and resilience, these qualities can also be developed and nurtured over time, indeed teaching these traits is the purpose of this book.

To cultivate catalyst qualities within oneself, individuals can start by identifying their personal strengths and areas for growth. This self-reflection enables one to understand better his or her potential in terms of igniting change and inspiring greatness. By having a growth mindset and seeking continuous learning opportunities, people are able to acquire the foundational skills needed for becoming transformational leaders.

One way in which someone can develop himself, or herself into a catalyst is by actively searching for challenges and seeing them as chances for growth. Taking new projects or responsibilities beyond comfort zones makes people stretch themselves so as to gain more knowledge, skills and experience; this risk taking spirit combined with uncertainty is what defines transformative leaders acting as catalysts for change.

Also important in the process of developing your leadership capabilities is cultivating self-awareness. By knowing your strengths, weaknesses, values, motives one can align their actions with their core principles hence inspiring others through authenticity when leading. Awareness about oneself helps leaders adapt to different situations in an inclusive empowering manner.

To nurture others' catalyst potential is also as important as fostering a culture of transformational leadership within organizations. This means looking for people who show the qualities of catalysts, like being passionate, creating new things and having an attitude of working hard to excel in their work. Organizations can therefore create a community of catalysts by giving such people opportunities for growth, mentorship and empowerment.

Furthermore, nurturing catalyst potential requires the creation of a supportive environment that promotes risk taking, innovation and collaboration. Leaders can establish open channels of communication where ideas are shared and experimented with; they can also celebrate both individual achievements as well as those achieved collectively. Thus, when organizations have cultures that value rewarding catalyst behaviors, they can maximize on their employees' strengths leading to transformative change.

Accordingly, this book looks at some important characteristics related to transformational leaders that will help you on this journey; particularly vision determination and communication skills.

Chapter 3

CHARACTERISTICS OF TRANSFORMATIONAL LEADERS: VISION, DETERMINATION, AND COMMUNICATION SKILLS

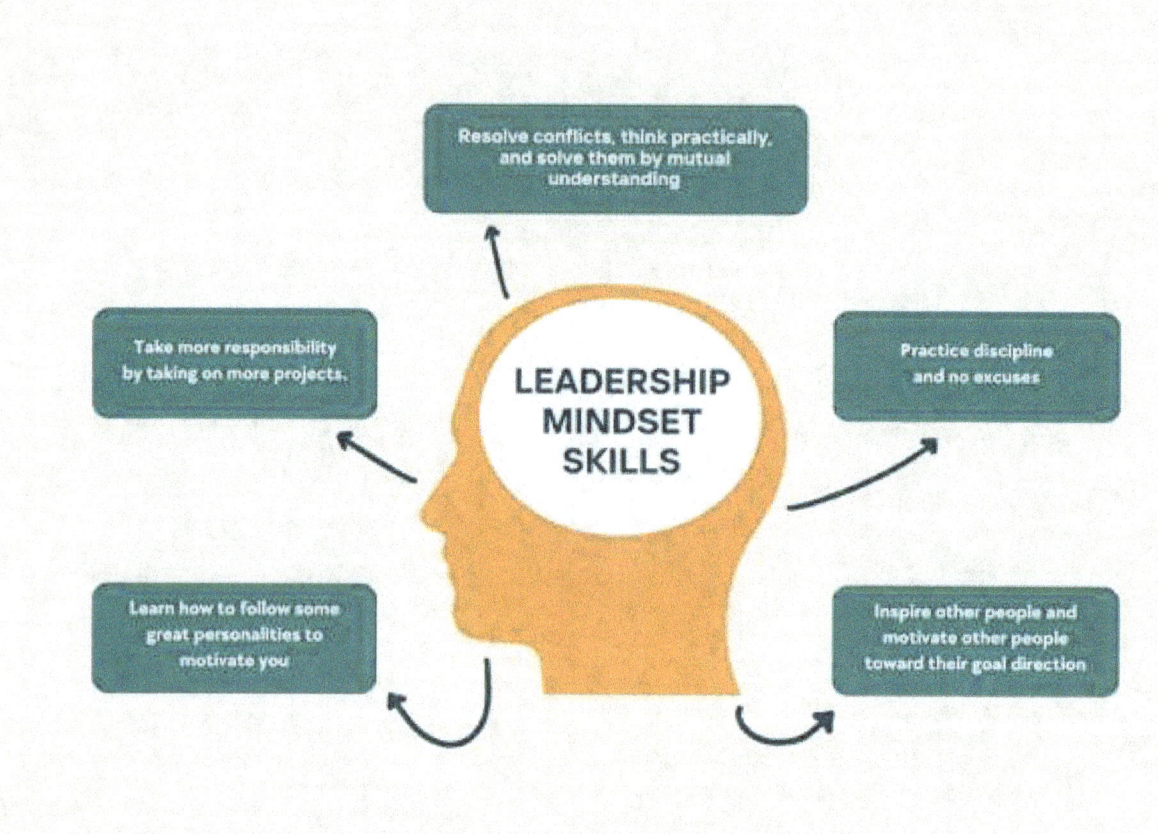

Transformational leaders have a clear and inspiring vision. By being able to see a better future for themselves, these leaders are able to put it into words that will be understood by followers. A compelling vision acts as a guiding beacon for individuals towards achieving common goals.

A transformational leader's vision is not just about setting goals or targets but goes beyond that; it has a broader purpose behind it which inspires people out of their current circumstances towards something greater. Communicated effectively by the leader, the vision creates an organizational sense of direction, purpose, and unity.

Mahatma Gandhi was one such catalyst. An example who had an indomitable spirit coupled with powerful visions; his aim being complete freedom from British rule in India an aim which ultimately attracted millions to his call and beginning the collapse of the British empire. He envisioned a country where everyone would live together peacefully without fear or prejudice but instead united under justice, peace and tolerance.

Steve jobs was another visionary leader whose style revolutionized the technology industry through driving production and design changes at apple Inc. Steve believed that products should be user-friendly while maintaining technological advancement, making it easier for people to interact with them on a daily basis. His obsession with design and aesthetics made apple products iconic thereby creating a customer base that shared his vision of a seamless integration between technology and everyday life.

On the other hand; transformational leaders should also understand that making a clear and inspiring vision doesn't mark the end, but rather the beginning of the journey. In this case therefore, it becomes imperative for them to ensure their visions align with their followers' values and aspirations as well. This fosters ownership among individuals who actively participate in realizing the shared goal.

In addition, visionary leaders must also possess good communication skills in order to effectively pass across their messages towards shaping the future 'their way'. They use persuasive language; storytelling techniques as well as compelling narratives through which they engage and inspire their followers. Therefore, transformational leaders excel at painting images of what lies ahead illustrating both the benefits that accrue from such actions alongside possibilities and potential challenges, together with a solution focused mindset.

Transformational leaders drive their organizations towards ambitious goals by creating a sense of urgency and purpose. They understand that a powerful vision not only motivates individuals but also provides a roadmap for success. Through their authentic belief in the vision, these leaders instil confidence, inspire innovation, and foster a culture of continuous improvement.

Transformational leaders hold the key to driving lasting organizational change, this is important as they are critical when it comes to resilience to challenges, active problem solving and driving organizational change that lasts. Although having a clear vision is essential, it is the unwavering determination of the leader that propels them forward enabling them to overcome obstacles on the path to achieving their vision.

We will look at how these leaders navigate through adversity with determination highlighting challenges and setbacks often faced by transformational leaders. For instance; people who have shown exceptional perseverance despite obstacles in real-life situations inspiring others to follow suit.

Aspiring transformational leaders can harness their own resilience and perseverance by understanding the role of determination in driving lasting change so that they can overcome obstacles on their leadership journey too. Readers will learn how they can cultivate determination within themselves using various tools thus fostering a resilient mindset which will enable them to achieve their specific transformative visions.

Creating an environment for collaboration and team success: effective communication skills for transformational leaders:

Transformational leadership requires effective communication skills because communication serves as the cornerstone of transformational leadership. Effective communication enables leaders to articulate their vision, inspire others, and create a sense of purpose and direction within their organizations. Transformational leaders possess exceptional communication skills that allow them to connect with their followers, share their ideas persuasively, and motivate them to achieve shared goals.

Let's explore the essential communication skills needed for transformational leadership as well as discuss the power of persuasive and inspiring communication in influencing others. Additionally; we will provide practical techniques for improving your communication skills as a transformational leader.

1. Active listening:

The importance of active listening is understood by transformational leaders who strive to truly hear and understand the perspectives, concerns, or ideas put forward by their followers. By actively listening; leaders demonstrate empathy thereby creating safe spaces where open dialogues can take place thus fostering trust through collaboration within an inclusive culture.

Transformational leaders can enhance active listening skills by practicing techniques such as maintaining eye contact, asking clarifying questions or summarizing/paraphrasing what others say. These practices not only make followers feel heard but also ensure that leaders fully grasp their viewpoints.

2. Storytelling:

Storytelling is a powerful tool used by transformational leaders in order to communicate their vision effectively with an engaging and relatable manner. Leaders are able to convey complex ideas through stories while evoking emotions thereby inspiring action too. For example; stories capture attention enabling followers to visualize possibilities while at the same time creating a sense of shared purpose among them.

Crafting stories that resonate with the audience, emphasizing personal experiences or anecdotes that relate to the organization's goals can develop transformative leaders' storytelling skills. By including features such as vivid descriptions, emotional appeal and clear messages, these individuals can captivate their listeners hence effectively communicating their vision.

3. Nonverbal communication:

Nonverbal cues have a great influence on communication and can determine how people understand information. Transformational leaders are mindful of their body language, facial expressions and tone of voice to ensure they match their intended message. Enthusiasm is conveyed through non-verbal signals like gestures, postures while sincerity is shown by maintaining eye contact.

In order to improve nonverbal communication skills it is important for transformational leaders to practice mirror imaging by copying what others do or say in a bid to establish rapport and build trust among them; they can also observe their postures/gestures/facial expressions so as not come off as closed off or uninviting.

4. Clear and inspiring communication:

Transformational leaders possess excellent skills in expressing their vision clearly and inspiringly. They use simple words that everyone understands when explaining complex issues so that they are easily grasped by all levels within an organization. They also communicate with passion, enthusiasm, and conviction which help energize and motivate followers.

To enhance clarity and inspiration in their communication style transformational leaders need to use simple concrete language instead of jargon terms; they may also bring their key message alive by means of visual aids or storytelling techniques gained from for example, taking a creative writing class or online course; additionally repetition of key phrases can be used together with metaphorical examples creating vivid images thus making stories more effective than just rephrasing the vision again and again without any alterations made whatsoever.

5. Feedback and recognition:

Effective communication requires timely feedback provision as well as recognition accorded towards subordinates by superiors. Transformational leaders who understand the importance of celebrating achievements alongside providing realistic constructive criticisms support personal growth and development respectively regular channels for feedback enable the tailoring of business practices brining 'everyone on board'.

To enhance feedback and recognition transformational leaders should engage in regular one-on-one meetings with their team members where they discuss progress issues pertaining to their performance. Moreover such individuals can acknowledge individual team achievements publicly either during departmental meetings or through written correspondence showing gratitude towards their efforts which further boosts engagement and promoting better results.

These essential communication skills are honed by transformational leaders to inspire others towards embracing change, fostering collaboration and achieving outstanding outcomes. Effective communication acts as a catalyst for transformational leadership connecting leaders with followers in pursuit of success together.

Inspiring others through authenticity and transparency:

In the world of transformational leadership, authenticity and transparency are two priceless qualities that can greatly affect not just how a leader relates with his or her followers but also the overall success of an organization or community at large. When leaders communicate with authenticity and transparency, they build trust, foster commitment, and inspire others to join them on their journey towards positive change.

Authenticity is about being who you truly are as a person. A leader who embodies this characteristic does not mind showing weakness while allowing their personal beliefs to shine through their leadership style. Being genuine yourself makes it possible for other people around you to feel comfortable being themselves too thus playing on your strengths naturally. Authenticity by its very nature involves open and 'transparent' communication.

Open communication, involves transparency and honesty. It means sharing information openly, explaining decisions made, and being responsible for what one does. Therefore, when leaders practice transparency they are able to build a sense of trust and make their colleagues feel valued.

Transparent communication is vital in building trust as it eliminates ambiguity thereby enabling employees to understand clearly what a leader wants from them as well as his strategies and expectations. When leaders share information openly, they show that they believe in their followers' ability to handle such pieces of information effectively leading to informed decision making. This makes the workers feel empowered to do their work accordingly.

Transparency also promotes commitment among teams. In this case leaders should let team members know about the goals set by an organization, challenges experienced and how far they have gone in achieving them so that it creates a sense of purpose which unites all people within the organization.

To become an authentic and transparent transformative leader takes deliberate effort. Here are some tips on how one can develop these qualities:

1. Redefine vulnerability: see vulnerability as an opportunity to connect with others instead of a sign of weakness. Share your thoughts, feelings and challenges authentically with your audience and encourage your followers to do the same.
2. Be an example leader: show transparency by giving out information freely, admitting the challenges you experience and making decisions together with your followers. Take responsibility for any errors and let your team members contribute their ideas.
3. Promote trust in how we communicate: encourage open communication, active listening, respect for diverse perspectives, and other trust-building mechanisms that create a conducive environment for trust creation. Encourage dialogue, collaboration and sharing of ideas and opinions.

4. Write clearly: use simple language without jargon or unnecessary terminology so that people can understand what you mean immediately after they read it. Be aware of nonverbal cues while actively listening to others' point of view.
5. Participate in active listening: authenticity and transparency require listening attentively to others without judgement on what they say or feel like. Seek to understand their perspectives on certain matters then give them space for expression.

Embracing authenticity and transparency as a transformative leader will enable others to fully engage in their work; build strong trust relationships among team members; create environments where sustainable change is possible through open communication as well as genuine expression; develop cultures that value every individual's input towards achieving shared visions.

Developing emotional intelligence to connect with followers:

Transformational leaders are aware of how emotional intelligence helps them form meaningful bonds with their followers. By showing empathy towards their subordinates' issues, transformational leaders can make a change within themselves that could be mirrored by others at large thereby creating an enabling environment for continued growth both personally & professionally (agarwal et al., 2018).

Acknowledging emotional intelligence should start from within ourselves as leaders because we cannot guide other people if we do not know who we are. A good leader should have a clear understanding about his/her strengths and weaknesses; this will enable him/her to know how emotions affect their leadership style as well as interaction with others (bass & riggio, 2006).

Consequently, it is important for a leader to understand their followers' feelings too. Therefore, transformational leaders listen carefully while observing both verbal and nonverbal cues in order to capture underlying emotions behind what is being said by their subjects (bass & riggio, 2006). Transformative leaders also empathize with their subordinates' experiences thereby showing commitment towards supporting and uplifting them within the organization/team which promotes the trust building process as well as fostering a sense of belonging amongst team-members.

To develop emotional intelligence as a transformational leader, there are several strategies to consider:

1. Reflect on yourself: find time regularly to think about your own emotions, reactions and behaviors. Ask yourself questions like "what triggered me feeling this way?" Or "how did my actions affect others?" This will help you understand yourself better including how certain moods influence your leadership skills.
2. Request for feedback: actively seek comments from team members or close friends regarding how well you demonstrate emotional intelligence. You may ask them about their opinions concerning your ability in understanding and managing emotions as well. Be open minded when receiving criticism since it can give you some areas for improvement (agarwal et al., 2018).
3. Empathy is developed through putting yourself in other people's shoes and trying to understand how they feel, think and experience life. You should also practice active listening and show genuine interest in their stories. Being empathetic creates a space where individuals are appreciated and known for who they are.
4. Self-regulation is about managing your own emotions effectively, especially when faced with challenging situations. Some strategies include deep breathing exercises, mindfulness meditation techniques or pausing before responding. Regulating emotions helps you to think before you act thus maintaining productive and positive relationships.
5. Social skills can be improved by enhancing interpersonal communication abilities that allow you to engage followers more effectively. This involves actively listening when others speak, telling stories effectively, and communicating clearly and honestly within the group. In addition, seek out opportunities for partnership working as well as team building activities that foster trust and cooperation.

In this way transformational leaders can connect with their followers on a deeper level if they have emotional intelligence too. This connection fosters trust, loyalty and commitment resulting into lasting change within the organization or community at large.

The role of catalysts in fostering innovation and creativity:

Remember that catalysts as defined within the transformational leadership context refer to individuals who possess unique qualities that enable them inspire positive change among teams or organizations. They serve as drivers of innovation by igniting sparks which propel their followers into higher levels of performance. However, catalysts go beyond usual expectations by pushing boundaries; questioning norms thereby creating an environment where fresh ideas are nurtured.

These transformative leaders are not just managers but visionaries because they see potentials within their teams which lie untapped until unlocked exhaustively by them alone tirelessly working towards its realization. They know that genuine progress comes from getting others to think differently; take risks; embrace unconventional approaches etc., hence contributing towards fostering an innovative culture / climate characterized by creativity.

In essence, catalysts act as agents of change who challenge traditional patterns of thought in order to move organizations forward. They can never be afraid of questioning old practices or even conventional wisdom while looking for opportunities aimed at growth and improvement. It is therefore necessary that creative abilities among team members are unleashed so as to drive innovations; improve problem solving capacities as well as ensure the overall success of the organization.

One major characteristic that defines a catalyst is being open to new ideas and perspectives. They possess an inquisitive mind and embrace different viewpoints knowing that it may take combining two or more concepts for something innovative come up. These people are always searching for opportunities where they can learn from others because they believe strongly in collaboration between individuals as well as exchange ideas among themselves thus valuing diversity; hence creating an environment conducive for creative thinking through being inclusive-mindedness .

Risk taking is also a characteristic that distinguishes catalysts. Catalysts will challenge the status quo without any fear or intimidation. Catalysts know that for progress to happen, one has to step out of their comfort zone and embrace uncertainty. They are also ready to take calculated risks and encourage the same in their teams. Catalysts create cultures where failure is embraced as an opportunity for experimentation and learning.

Catalysts are characterized by an open mindset and a willingness to take chances, but they also have strong purpose-driven passion that drives them forward relentlessly believing in positive change possibilities which others can ignore. Others are inspired by their unflinching determination beyond limits imposed upon them, encouraging creative thinking and striving towards perfection.

Moreover, catalysts are excellent communicators with exceptional language skills. Their visions can be clearly expressed and others can be encouraged to participate in those dreams. Therefore, these leaders use storytelling along with well-told stories as effective means of conveying ideas capturing audiences' imaginations creating enthusiasm amongst listeners. They communicate in ways that people find motivating while still being able to inspire collective ownership.

Catalysts foster an environment of creativity by embodying certain qualities; as a result, they cultivate innovation among employees within an organization. They become key models who help individuals think differently, challenge assumptions and contribute unique perspectives thereby empowering the team members thereof. Through their leadership styles, these people motivate others towards achieving common goals hence creating a culture of innovation necessary for organizational success.

Chapter 4

THE ROLE OF CATALYSTS IN FOSTERING INNOVATION AND CREATIVITY:

HIGHLIGHTING REAL-WORLD EXAMPLES OF TRANSFORMATIVE LEADERS WHO LEVERAGED CATALYSTS:

This section will explore stories about influential leaders who have used catalysts effectively to promote innovation and creativity within their respective organizations. When we look at these real-life examples, we can understand more deeply what facilitated this leadership style necessary for new ideas to emerge and for employees to think outside the box.

Digital catalysts are different from traditional leaders because they flourish in an ever-changing world filled with uncertainties. They fully understand the power that lies behind innovation and recognize that change is a prerequisite for survival in today's fast-paced society.

Accordingly catalysts, possess a unique combination of traits that separates them from others. They are visionary individuals who constantly seek out fresh opportunities while imagining things which other people cannot perceive. They are incredible at making connections between unrelated ideas using various knowledge bases and experiences to come up with revolutionary solutions.

Moreover, catalysts demonstrate exceptional resilience as well as adaptability to digital and technological. These people embrace ambiguity; they take risks far beyond traditional boundaries so that bold new paths may occur, yet still have strategies in place to manage that risk. Understanding setbacks often constitute learning experiences rather than stumbling blocks towards progression and failure is not seen as an outcome but a stepping stone to success.

Some of the important qualities of effective digital catalysts include strong communication skills and an ability to unite teams behind a common vision while empowering individuals towards delivering their diverse perspectives. They foster collaboration by encouraging open discussions among team members thereby promoting an environment where heterogeneous thoughts can thrive and empower less digitally adept team-members to learn new skills and information in an open rewarding environment, in a 'technology first' culture.

There is no overstating how significant catalysts are in the digital era. As technology continues disrupting industries and changing how we work, it is only through such leaders like them that we find direction amid all this uncertainty. Such individuals act as agents on behalf of organizations guiding them through transformational journeys leading people into adopting innovative practices.

Come join us as we unlock the power of catalysts on this thrilling adventure into tomorrow's transformational leaders within rapidly changing digital landscapes. Collectively, let us embrace changes, challenge traditions and build an innovative future.

The role of catalysts in the digital age:

Organizations across different sectors face unique challenges and opportunities posed by the digital age. The landscape is characterized by uncertainty due to rapid innovation, technological advancements, evolving consumer expectations among others. In this regard, catalysts play a key role in fostering innovation and creativity.

As previously discussed a catalyst is a person who can bring about change by challenging established norms and encouraging others to think outside the box. What sets aside a digital catalyst is there ability to stay ahead of trends and implement new and existing technologies in an interesting and creative way. They do not want things to stay as they are but rather look for new possibilities and ways of doing things differently. In an era where adaptability and agility are critical factors for success; catalysts become indispensable leaders guiding their organizations through complex transformations.

Perhaps one of the main reasons why these individuals are important in today's digital world is because they can navigate through uncertain times better than anyone else could ever do so naturally. There are times when organizations find themselves in ambiguous situations due to rapidly changing technologies or market dynamics where there might not be any clear answer or known solution. Catalysts thrive under these circumstances because they have a natural inclination towards embracing ambiguity and exploring unchartered territories.

Furthermore, catalysts have a deeper understanding of the potential opportunities that digital advancements present. These disruptions can be used to change organizations by pushing them to think differently about their strategies and innovate in order to stay competitive as stated by them. Catalysts inspire teams by challenging old ways of doing things and encouraging them to think outside the box, making them explore new ideas, experiment with emerging technologies and come up with new ways of solving problems.

In addition, catalysts are key in promoting collaboration and open-mindedness within organizations. They value different opinions from people hence encourage individuals not to fear when expressing their thoughts and views on matters affecting the organization. In this kind of environment, teams are able to think beyond boundaries thus bringing about innovative ideas while drawing upon collective intelligence and creativity from their members.

Moreover, continuous learning and growth is something catalysts understand very well. Their aim is to see that individuals expand their skill sets through embracing new technologies while at the same time staying updated on industry trends. A growth mindset which is one of the responsibilities they carry motivates teams into seeking knowledge so as they can reach for higher levels in terms of self-improvement.

Ultimately, digital catalysts are change agents who drive innovation and creativity in today's digital age. They know what it means for businesses or any entity operating under uncertainty and possible obsolescence; it requires challenging what has been done before thinking outside boxes about how things could be done differently such that success may still prevail amidst rapid changes occurring within environments. With these unique qualities being leveraged upon by such people, organizations end up realizing their full potentials thereby shaping an innovative and successful future for themselves.

Case studies: highlighting catalysts in action:

In this section, readers will dive deep into real-world case studies showing how catalysts drive innovation and creativity. We highlight successful catalysts across different industries who have brought transformative changes.

One such example involves Sarah Thompson who was a catalyst in a private healthcare industry setting. Instead of focusing only on doctors' needs in a difficult time-sensitive environment, sarah realized that patients must come first; hence she introduced ai-driven technologies and data analytics into her organization. Her team used artificial intelligence to go through patient feedbacks, identify patterns and develop personalized treatment plans free-ing up much needed clinician time and thus revolutionizing care provision without jeopardizing health outcomes. Through this vision accompanied by challenging existing norms within her workplace; Sarah acted as a digital catalyst for positive change.

Another case study is about James Ramirez who played a similar role in the technology sector. He saw how ai could disrupt traditional business models leading to innovation within companies like his own. Thus, he advocated for its adoption thereby resulting in an ai-powered human resources and customer service chatbot that supported a previously over-run personal department. It not only made work easier but also gave customers and staff personalized experiences thus enhancing their satisfaction levels and loyalty through improved services, sign-posting, and effective gatekeeping. James's ability to inspire his team towards embracing ai-driven solutions shows how catalysts ignite creativity while fostering innovation.

These are just a few out of many other examples which demonstrate huge effects brought about by catalysts when it comes to driving transformative changes. Through such stories, readers get insights on strategies used by successful catalysts as well as overcoming obstacles in order to achieve significant outcomes.

It is important to note that every case study represents different approaches and outcomes which ensures that the reader gets a full grasp of how catalysts can drive innovation and creativity in many ways. These are real-life examples that will inspire readers to become catalysts themselves.

Strategies on becoming a digital catalyst:

In this section, you will find out some practical strategies and techniques for becoming a successful digital catalyst. It goes beyond just understanding what a digital catalyst is but gives insights on how one can develop his or her leadership skills, cultivate an innovative mindset and empower others to accept change.

One way to do it is to concentrate on your personal growth during the age of digitalization. Leaders have to keep improving themselves as well as broaden their knowledge in technology for them to be considered as catalysts. They can do this by attending seminars or workshops, seeking learning opportunities from other people who are knowledgeable about new trends within their industries, among other ways by staying updated with what is happening around them within these sectors. Additionally, when leaders invest in their personal development journey they serve as role models inspiring those around them towards achieving the same. Many universities offer free courses through websites like: Harvard education (search for catalogue free), or the open university.

Another strategy is fostering a culture of innovation within organizations. This means creating an environment where out-of-the-box thinking is encouraged and celebrated. For example, leaders should provide resources such as funding for innovative ideas; they could also promote collaboration through cross-functional teams while setting aside time specifically meant for brainstorming sessions among others. By doing so leaders cultivate an innovative culture that allows employees to think creatively hence driving change.

Overcoming resistance to change is another critical component of being a digital catalyst. Unlike other change catalysts, digital catalysts often have to deal with acute technophobia amongst the workforce. Change often meets opposition from individuals and organizations alike. Indeed the sheer act of implementing new technology itself, which undergoes teething problems during its initial implementation stages, can create technophobia in susceptible individuals. Therefore, being a digital catalyst requires leaders who can deal with resistance upfront thereby creating buy-in regarding new ideas/ projects as well as initiatives launched by them; these might involve effective communication as well as training explaining why there's a need for change; the effective involving of all stakeholders actively during decision making processes, and finally showing successful instances where creativity brought about innovation. To solve teething problems with technology employing, training and recruiting people with the correct skillset/mindset and technological expertise is necessary, while also avoiding or suspending cutting costs when implementing the new technology itself. In addition the proper optimization of contingency budgets should be in place with sufficient contingency funding to overcome obstacles.

In order to achieve this, potential change should be discussed with team members with the right skillset to advance potential problems *before* the implementation of the change itself, stakeholders should brainstorm problems and solutions amidst an atmosphere of no judgement and positive feedback.

Lastly, leaders need to know how they can promote creative thinking among their teams. This can be achieved by giving employees opportunities to explore new ideas and take risks through experimentation. It also involves coming up with platforms that allow sharing of ideas, implementing recognition programs for those who make innovative contributions as well as creating an environment where individuals feel safe enough to speak out their minds without fear of victimization.

Implementing these strategies will turn leaders into catalysts for digital change in their organizations. They will be able to inspire innovation, encourage creative thinking and empower their teams towards embracing change. Through these efforts they will unlock the full potential within themselves and drive a culture of ongoing innovation within their respective fields during an era of digitization and change.

Harnessing ai as a catalyst:

Let us now look at an exciting intersection between artificial intelligence (ai) and catalytic leadership more specifically. While catalysts are known for provoking change and inspiring innovation, ai itself acts as a catalyst - it augments human abilities making them better leaders.

Now, we will look at how leaders can integrate ai technologies into their processes to drive innovation and creativity in various ways. Ai has the potential to revolutionize traditional paradigms by providing valuable insights, accelerating decision-making processes, and spurring creative thinking among team members. Transformational leaders that embrace ai's power can unlock new possibilities for their organizations in uncharted territories.

However, there are important challenges that must be addressed before using ai as a catalyst. As ai continues to advance and become more sophisticated, leaders must navigate issues such as data privacy, algorithmic biases, and the impact on human workers. Leaders need to explore these challenges proactively so that they know how to deploy ai ethically and responsibly.

We will delve into more real-world examples to show how leaders have effectively harnessed ai as a catalyst for change. We will give practical strategies and insights on how organizations can leverage this technology to drive innovation and creativity within them. By finding the right balance between human intuition and machine capabilities, leaders can cultivate an environment that embraces the transformative power of ai while still maintaining the human touch necessary for true creativity.

Leaders have successfully harnessed the power of ai in transforming different sectors thereby showcasing its potential to revolutionize industries and spur innovation. An illustrative case is the use of ai at md anderson cancer center where ibm's watson system analyzed patient data thereby expediting diagnosis as well as treatment recommendations for certain cancers. Through this application not only did ai accelerate analysis of medical information but it also demonstrated how healthcare outcomes could be improved through artificial intelligence.

Ai has also been used in leadership training beyond healthcare so as to improve personalized learning experiences together with human decision-making ability. For example, generative ai creates custom-made leadership development programs which enable individuals to enhance their skills via interactive modules. By incorporating ai into leadership training organizations can provide more effective customized learning experiences leading professional growth and overall leadership improvement.

Moreover, strategic implementation empowers employees while optimizing managerial functions through ai. By automating routine tasks or providing data-driven insights, ai frees up middle managers' capacity for higher value leadership responsibilities such as strategic planning and people management.

This resource reallocation increases operational efficiency and fosters a dynamic organizational structure thereby highlighting how traditional leadership roles are transformed by ai.

Regions like Québec in Canada have become ai powerhouses nurturing a new crop of professionals and innovative companies that develop ai solutions. Québec's success can be attributed to strong ecosystem with vibrant ai community, collaborative partnerships between academia and industry as well as supportive environment for technology transfer & commercialization. This shows how effective regional leadership can leverage ai to drive economic growth, technological advancement, and societal progress.

Effective deployment of ai as a catalyst for change is seen in diverse contexts ranging from healthcare to leadership development or regional economic growth. These examples underscore ai's transformative potential in driving innovation, improving decision-making, reshaping traditional business practices thereby emphasizing the crucial role played by leaders when it comes to leveraging ai for positive change.

As we wrap up examining the potential of catalysts in the digital age, this section acts as a connector between catalytic leadership and technological advances which define our current world. With an understanding of how ai can serve as a catalyst on its own, leaders can fully embrace the possibilities for innovation and creativity in our ever more digital world.

Chapter 5

CREATING AN ENVIRONMENT THAT PROMOTES COLLABORATION AND TEAM SUCCESS

This next step is crucial for the best transformational leaders. In this section, we will explore practical techniques for fostering a collaborative culture within organizations, with a focus on the leader's role in setting the tone and expectations for collaboration and effective teamwork, a critical part of any leadership and management role.

Collaboration is much more than simply working together; it holds the key to unlocking the true potential of teams and organizations. By harnessing the collective intelligence, skills, and experiences of individuals, collaborations can drive innovation, foster creativity, and achieve remarkable results.

Throughout history, numerous examples illustrate the power of collaboration in transforming industries, advancing scientific discoveries, and overcoming complex challenges. One such example is the apollo 11 moon landing mission, where the collaborative efforts of astronauts, engineers, scientists, and countless others made an unprecedented leap for humankind possible.

Organizations that prioritize collaboration not only benefit from increased productivity and efficiency but also experience improved employee engagement and satisfaction. When individuals feel empowered to contribute their unique perspectives and ideas, they become more invested in the success of the team and organization as a whole.

On the other hand, absence of collaboration can be detrimental to individuals', teams' and entire organizations' health. Missed opportunities, stagnation, and decreased morale could result from siloed thinking along with a lack of communication and increased territorial behavior. Today's rapidly changing world requires organizations that embrace interconnectedness as well as interdependence hence those which do not risk being left behind by failing to foster collaboration in the digital age.

We will explore how effective leadership plays a pivotal role in creating an environment that supports collaboration. We will delve into key principles and strategies necessary for cultivating a culture of collaboration within organizations. Readers will be provided insights on how to overcome barriers through highlighting real life examples of successful collaborations thereby giving them the knowledge and tools needed to unleash their transformational power within their teams and organizations.

As we embark on this journey towards understanding collaboration catalysts and effective leadership practices let us recognize the immense potential that lies within our collective efforts. Together, we can unlock new levels of success and make lasting contributions to our organizations and the world at large. The role of effective leadership in fostering collaboration is crucial in creating an environment conducive to collaboration and effective teamwork. Effective leaders possess specific qualities and skills that enable them to drive collaboration within teams and organizations alike.

One key quality of effective leaders is strong communication skills. They are able to clearly articulate their vision for collaboration, ensuring that team members understand their goals and objectives. Leaders create a shared understanding and purpose through open transparent communication with team members thus fostering collaboration at its most basic level.

Another important skill of effective leaders is an ability to build trust. Trust is a prerequisite for successful collaboration as it makes a team member feel secure enough sharing his/her ideas to take risks without fearing judgment from others within their respective teams or departments, while leaders who consistently act openly and communicate as well as genuinely empathize are more likely to develop a business culture where employees will be willing to collaborate and give their all.

Strong interpersonal skills are also possessed by effective transformational leaders, who help to navigate conflicts and facilitate effective collaboration. They manage various personalities, settle disputes between people and encourage healthy dialogue. This will facilitate collaboration since it creates a positive environment where all voices are respected.

For those who want to become leaders, they can find inspiration from real-life examples of leaders who have successfully promoted collaboration. For example, nelson mandela showed exceptional leadership during his tenure as president of south africa when he promoted collaboration and acceptance. His inclusive leadership style led to the reconciliation of different groups ultimately leading to the end of apartheid and the birth of democracy.

In the business world, tim cook is known for his inclusive leadership approach that encourages team collaboration at apple inc. Under cook's direction cross-functional teams have been established that has resulted in new innovative products such as ios17 and the newest version of the apple watch.

These examples show how effective leaders can drive collaboration through their actions, communication and inclusive leadership styles. In order for future leaders to establish a collaborative culture within their own teams or organizations they must emulate these qualities and learn key strategies to attain success and meet their objectives for change. The relationship between collaboration & effective leadership is crucial for driving team success. By prioritizing & actively supporting it, leaders create an environment that promotes innovation, creativity & synergy among team members without discrimination based on age or gender differences. Good leaders recognize that working together should not just be mere coexistence but rather synergized diverse perspectives towards a shared goal and achievement.

Collaboration requires strong leadership practices that facilitate and encourage collaboration within teams. Thus, leaders who embrace open communication will allow a free flow of ideas from team members while active listening ensures all participants contribute equally regardless of one's position in society; also inclusivity creates room for individuals' thoughts being heard without fear or favoritism among others things they do well namely recognizing value each person adds due to unique viewpoint thereby ensuring everyone feels heard valued equally throughout this whole process.

Leaders can further enhance collaboration within teams by leading by example, demonstrating the importance of collaboration through their actions and decisions. Leaders actively participating in collaborative efforts set the tone for teamwork and show their commitment to achieving collective success.

Leaders can also establish clear expectations for collaboration with an emphasis on it being a core value within the organization. This includes setting goals that require cross-functional collaboration and recognizing reward systems that promote collaborative behavior as well. In this way leaders align incentives with desired behaviors which encourage team members' effective working together.

In addition, effective leaders can create opportunities for collaboration through structured processes or platforms. They can encourage team members to engage in cross-functional projects where diverse skill-sets may be combined for maximum impact while providing resources & support needed like tools used during collaboration or even programs such as interpersonal skills enhancement training.

By fostering a collaborative culture within teams, leaders empower individuals to share open ideas while maintaining trust as well as respect among themselves. They should encourage healthy debate that allows constructive feedback so that different perspectives can be heard & integrated into decision-making processes.

Collaboration cannot exist without effective leadership; hence both should go hand in hand when driving team success.

A step by step approach:

The first stride towards creating a vision for collaborative success is to clearly describe the desired outcome or goal of collaboration. This could involve setting specific targets, identifying areas for improvement or envisioning a common achievement. By expressing this vision, leaders give direction and purpose to the team's collaborative efforts.

After establishing the vision, it is important for leaders to communicate it effectively to their members. This involves not only sharing what the vision is about but also explaining why it matters and what individuals gain from it as well as the whole organization. For leaders to inspire enthusiasm and a sense of belonging within team-members they must employ persuasive language.

Creating collaborative goals is the next step and another critical part of developing a vision for success. Leaders should work closely with their team members in order to set clear and measurable objectives which contribute towards the overall aim. Smart goals should be specific, measurable, attainable relevant time bound ensuring that they are challenging yet realistic.

Once these collaborative goals are established then there must be a roadmap made towards achieving them by the leader(s). This implies breaking down each goal into actionable steps/milestones assigning duties accordingly among team members who must deliver on them as planned through a structured plan provided by leaders so as to know how they fit in big picture of achieving this future state.

Establishment of a clear vision and purpose along with effective communication and setting up of collaborative goals with the creation of a time-specific roadmap constitute the most effective ways a transformational leader can inspire an atmosphere of collaboration with the organisation, but what about barriers to collaboration, overcoming them and teamwork more generally?

Overcoming barriers to collaboration:

Collaboration is a powerful tool for driving team success, but it's not always easy. There are common barriers and obstacles that can hinder collaboration within teams or organizations. However, with the right strategies and techniques, these barriers can be overcome.

One common barrier to collaboration is poor communication. When team members do not communicate effectively with each other, it results in misunderstandings misalignment breakdowns in collaboration. Leaders can overcome this barrier by fostering open and transparent communication through establishing clear channels for sharing ideas and feedback such as regular team meetings, virtual collaboration tools or dedicated spaces for informal conversations.

Another obstacle towards effective teamwork lies in a lack of trust among team members. Trust is crucial because it enables individuals to freely express their views without any fear of victimization from fellow colleagues or superiors. To build trust leaders should start by being trustworthy themselves thus setting an example while at the same time creating an environment where trustworthiness is promoted hence promoting accountability, recognition of individual contributions and effective conflict resolution.

Collaboration can also be hindered by conflicting interests and competing priorities. For example, when team members have different goals or priorities, it may be difficult to find a common ground for collaboration. Therefore, effective leaders can overcome this barrier through facilitating open discussions. They should encourage compromise and consensus-building wherever possible.

Another factor that can help in overcoming these barriers is creating a culture that encourages collaboration. In other words, leaders need to create psychological safety zones where individuals feel comfortable taking risks as well as promoting inclusivity and recognizing and valuing diverse perspectives; with the encouragement of constructive feedback and dialogue, with rules practices and corporate policies all in alignment.

By addressing these barriers leaders can create an environment where teams work effectively together unleashing the full potential of their organizations. Thus, through improved communication, building trust, addressing conflicting interests and fostering a collaborative culture, barriers can be overcome enabling teams to collaborate more effectively towards shared goals.

Optimizing teamwork and collaboration: a comprehensive guide:

Teamwork and collaboration have become essential for organizations to thrive in today's fast-paced business environment. A teams' ability to work together effectively has a significant impact on their performance, productivity, and overall success. We will explore various aspects of teamwork and collaboration including different team structures, models for team effectiveness and strategies to foster more effective collaboration within different types of teams and the organization as a whole.

The success of any organization depends on teamwork and collaboration among its members. When people come together with their skills, knowledge, resources they achieve common goals more efficiently than if each individual acted alone. However, cooperation is not the only element of collaboration; rather it involves active participation in decision-making process as well as communication among team members with a willingness towards achieving a shared objective. Today's complex business landscape requires organizations to rely on teams who can handle tough projects and drive innovation or change.

The concept of collaboration:

The word "collaboration" comes from two Latin words: "com-" meaning "with", and "laborer" which means "to work". Collaboration involves more than just cooperation; it includes components such as leadership, decentralized decision making and a sense of shared purpose. When teams collaborate effectively, they can leverage their differences in order to enhance problem solving skills and create an innovative atmosphere.

Understanding team structures:

Teams can take different forms depending on their specific characteristics and dynamics. Understanding these structures will help organizations optimize their teamwork efforts. Here are some common types of teams:

Dedicated teams:

Dedicated teams consist of individuals who are fully committed to a specific project or objective within an organization. Such teams work tirelessly towards achieving their goals and often possess high levels of expertise in relevant fields. The dedication and focus exhibited by members of dedicated teams contribute significantly towards effectiveness as well as successful completion for projects in general.

Project teams:

These are temporary groups formed around time-sensitive tasks or projects; they bring together people with diverse skills and knowledge from different areas or departments so that they can work together towards achieving one common purpose . Project teams usually have a project manager who provides guidance during execution stage thereby necessitating efficient communication among all team members for coordination purposes leading into fruitful outcomes.

Self-managed or self-organizing teams:

Self-organized or self-managed teams do not have an official leader; instead, they are collectively responsible for the performance and decision making process. Collaboration, trust, and common objectives are some of the factors that make them successful. By allowing every individual to bring in their own unique skills and viewpoints, such teams can create a culture of collaboration as well as accountability.

Virtual teams:

Virtual teams are groups of people who work together on a common task despite being geographically dispersed. Technological advancements have made it possible for these teams to communicate effectively even though they are physically separated from each other. Virtual teams have to use good communication skills; effective collaboration tools should also be utilized while setting goals that everyone understands so as to overcome distance problems.

Operational teams:

Operational teams are responsible for managing the everyday affairs of a business or organization. They ensure smooth operations of systems and processes leading to improved efficiency levels across all departments within an organization. To maintain quality outputs, meet deadlines and optimize performance results within operational teams requires effective collaboration.

Problem-solving teams:

Problem-solving teams are created to tackle specific issues or challenges faced by organizations. These groups involve individuals with different backgrounds coming up with innovative solutions together through sharing ideas collaboratively. A problem solving team requires cooperation for creativity as well as analyzing multiple points of view before deciding on what course should be taken.

Informal teams:

Informal teams arise spontaneously among employees who share common interests beyond the formal structure of a company or institution. Informal groups may also develop naturally when people collaborate on projects outside their regular areas of work responsibility (hill & jones 2010). This promotes creativity in organizations by encouraging cross-functional collaboration among members resulting into increased camaraderie amongst colleagues working together towards achieving certain goals.

Leadership teams:

A leadership team is composed mainly of top executives and senior managers within an enterprise who set strategic directions, make important decisions on behalf of the organization and drive its overall performance levels. Different goals can be aligned through collaboration among members, sharing insights with one another and ensuring that decisions are made effectively.

Working teams:

Working teams are generally those that exist within an organization to meet particular objectives or goals on a continuous basis (hayes, 2010). These teams consist of members from different departments or functional areas who come together in order to perform shared tasks. For effective coordination, knowledge sharing and achievement of desired outcomes; there has to be a collaborative environment within working teams.

Special purpose teams:

Special purpose teams are created for specific purposes/projects outside regular operational duties. Often temporary in nature aimed at achieving specific objectives within defined time frames. In special purpose teams, individuals bring in their unique skills/views enabling them work towards attaining project goals efficiently through collaboration.

Multi-functional teams:

Cross-functional or multifunctional teams are composed of people from various departments within an organization. They bring together different skills and backgrounds to achieve a common goal (hill & jones 2010). Integrating diverse perspectives is important for leveraging specialized knowledge while achieving holistic solutions within multi-functional groups through collaboration.

Matrix teams:

In matrix organizational structures, employees have multiple reporting relationships including solid lines (direct reporting) and dotted lines (indirect/flexible reporting). In some cases, individuals may hold two positions simultaneously working on two different projects at the same time thus making it possible for them to perform both functions concurrently within matrix structures. Complex reporting relationships require collaboration among members so as to ensure efficient management across various projects while maximizing resource utilization levels in these groups.

Different team structures enable collaboration to take place in diverse ways within organizations. Each team structure requires specific strategies and practices to maximize collaboration and harness the full potential of team members.

Why collaboration is important in teamwork:

In teamwork, collaboration plays a big role in optimizing and driving the success of the organization. When teams collaborate effectively, they can achieve the following benefits:

Improved communication:

Collaboration as we have talked about before improves communication in teams making it possible for individuals to exchange information, ideas and feedback more effectively. Effective communication is necessary for ensuring that team members are aligned with goals, tasks, and expectations. Collaboration promotes open and transparent communication which reduces misunderstandings, conflicts as well as inefficiencies.

Fostering innovation:

Collaboration fosters innovation through the exchange of different perspectives, ideas and experiences. When team members collaborate together they can tap into the collective knowledge base of their peers thus leading to more innovative solutions or approaches being developed by them all collectively. Collaboration creates an environment where creativity flourishes alongside risk-taking behaviours thereby promoting continuous improvement within organizations through innovation

Boosting efficiency:

Collaboration enables teams to work together towards a common goal, leveraging individual strengths and resources. When team members collaborate, they can divide tasks, share responsibilities, and leverage each other's expertise, leading to improved efficiency. Collaboration reduces duplication of efforts, streamlines processes, and enhances productivity within teams.

Driving overall team performance:

Effective collaboration enhances team dynamics, trust, and morale, leading to improved overall team performance. When team members collaborate, they feel a sense of ownership, engagement, and shared responsibility for the team's success. Collaboration fosters a supportive and inclusive work environment, where individuals can contribute their best work, leading to higher levels of satisfaction and motivation.

The clockwork concept: collaboration as the key component:

Team collaboration can be compared to the workings of a clockwork mechanism. In a clockwork, every component, no matter how small or seemingly insignificant, is essential for the smooth functioning of the overall system. Similarly, in a team, every member's skills, expertise, and input are necessary for the team's success. Collaboration within teams is the mechanism that brings all the components together, ensuring effective coordination, communication, and synergy.

Just as a clockwork mechanism relies on the harmonious movement of its parts, effective collaboration involves the synchronized efforts of team members. Collaboration enables teams to harness the collective power of their diverse skills, perspectives, and experiences, leading to better decision-making, problem-solving, and overall team performance.

Team effectiveness models: a framework for success:

To optimize teamwork and collaboration, organizations can leverage various team effectiveness models. These models provide a framework for understanding the factors that contribute to team success and offer strategies for enhancing collaboration within teams. Let's explore four popular team effectiveness models:

1. The Lencioni model:

The Lencioni model, based on Patrick Lencioni's book "the five dysfunctions of a team," identifies five common dysfunctions that hinder team effectiveness. These dysfunctions include absence of trust, fear of conflict, lack of commitment, avoidance of accountability, and inattention to results. The model emphasizes the importance of cultivating trust, resolving conflicts, fostering commitment, promoting accountability, and focusing on results to enhance team effectiveness.

2. The 7 model:

The t7 model, developed by Michael Lombardo and Robert exchanger, focuses on internal and external factors that influence team effectiveness. The model highlights the importance of factors such as trust, talent, team skills, task skills, team leader fit, and company support. Organizations can enhance team effectiveness by investing in developing these factors and creating a supportive environment for collaboration.

3. Tuckman's team development model:

The Tuckman team development model, developed by Bruce Tuckman, describes four stages of team development: forming, storming, norming, and performing. This model recognizes that teams go through a natural progression as they form, establish relationships, resolve conflicts, and achieve high performance. Team leaders can guide teams through these stages by providing clear goals, facilitating relationship-building, and encouraging collaboration.

4. Katzenbach and smith model:

The Katzenbach and smith model emphasizes the importance of team goals, skills, accountability, and commitment. This model suggests that teams should focus on performance results, work products, and personal growth to enhance collaboration and achieve success. Leaders can support collaboration by fostering a sense of community, providing coaching and training in collaboration skills, and promoting a culture of accountability and commitment.

By adopting these team effectiveness models, organizations can create a basis for collaboration and establish strategies to enhance teamwork and team performance. These models provide a framework for understanding the dynamics of effective teams and offer practical guidance for fostering collaboration within organizations.

Strategies to foster collaboration within teams:

To optimize teamwork and collaboration, organizations can implement various strategies that promote a collaborative culture and enhance team effectiveness. Here are eight practices for fostering collaboration within teams:

1. Invest in building social relationships:

Building and maintaining social relationships within the organization is crucial for fostering collaboration. Executives can invest in creating spaces and opportunities for employees to interact and connect with one another. For example, organizations can design office spaces that encourage spontaneous interactions, organize team-building events, and promote social activities that bring people together.

2. Model collaborative behavior:

Leaders play a vital role in shaping the culture of collaboration within teams. By modeling collaborative behavior, leaders set an example for others to follow. Executives can demonstrate collaboration by working together on projects, seeking input from team members, and promoting a culture of openness, respect, and inclusivity.

3. Use coaching to reinforce collaboration:

Coaching can be a powerful tool for reinforcing a collaborative culture within teams. Leaders can provide coaching and mentoring opportunities to help team members develop collaboration skills, enhance their communication abilities, and build relationships. Coaching can also help individuals understand the importance of collaboration and its impact on team performance and success.

4. Train employees in collaboration skills:

Collaboration requires specific skills such as appreciating others, engaging in purposeful conversations, resolving conflicts productively, and managing programs effectively. Organizations can provide training programs and workshops to equip employees with these skills. By investing in training, organizations can empower employees to collaborate more effectively and contribute their best to team goals.

5. Support a sense of community:

Creating a sense of community within teams can foster collaboration and a shared sense of purpose. Organizations can sponsor events, networking groups, and activities that bring team members together. These activities can range from social gatherings to team-building exercises and community service initiatives. By supporting a sense of community, organizations can strengthen relationships, build trust, and enhance collaboration within teams.

6. Allocate time for informal interactions:

Informal interactions can play a significant role in fostering collaboration within teams. Organizations can create opportunities for team members to connect and interact on a personal level. This can be done through informal coffee breaks, team lunches, or virtual social events. These informal interactions provide an avenue for team members to build relationships, share ideas, and collaborate in a relaxed and informal setting.

7. Encourage cross-functional collaboration:

Cross-functional collaboration allows teams to leverage diverse expertise and perspectives from different areas of the organization. Leaders can encourage cross-functional collaboration by creating opportunities for individuals from different departments or teams to work together on projects or initiatives. By bridging silos and promoting cross-functional collaboration, organizations can enhance innovation, problem-solving, and overall team effectiveness.

8. Foster a culture of learning and continuous improvement:

A culture of learning and continuous improvement is essential for fostering collaboration within teams. Organizations can create a safe and supportive environment where individuals are encouraged to share knowledge, learn from one another, and embrace new ideas. By promoting a culture of learning, organizations can enhance collaboration, creativity, and adaptability within teams.

By implementing these strategies, organizations can create a collaborative culture that empowers teams to work together effectively, drive innovation, and achieve their goals.

The role of transformational leadership in fostering collaboration:

Leadership plays a critical role in fostering collaboration within teams. Transformational leadership, characterized by inspiring and empowering team members, is particularly effective in promoting collaboration. Transformational leaders create a shared vision, motivate and inspire team members, and empower them to take ownership of their work. These leaders provide guidance, support, and resources to facilitate collaboration and create an environment where individuals can thrive.

Transformational leaders also encourage open communication, active listening, and two-way feedback within teams. They promote a culture of trust, respect, and psychological safety, where team members feel comfortable expressing their ideas and challenging the status quo. By fostering a collaborative culture and leading by example, transformational leaders can drive collaboration, enhance team performance, and create a positive work environment.

Teamwork and collaboration are essential for organizations striving for success in today's dynamic business landscape. By understanding different team structures, leveraging team effectiveness models, and implementing strategies to foster collaboration, organizations can optimize teamwork and enhance team performance. Collaboration enhances communication, fosters innovation, boosts efficiency, and drives overall team success.

Transformational leaders play a crucial role in fostering collaboration by modeling collaborative behavior, providing coaching and support, and creating a culture of collaboration. By investing in collaboration and empowering teams to work together effectively, organizations can achieve their goals, drive innovation, and stay ahead in a competitive market.

Remember, fostering collaboration is an ongoing process that requires continuous effort, adaptation, and improvement. By embracing collaboration as a core value and integrating it into the organizational culture, organizations can create a collaborative environment where teams thrive, individuals excel, and the overall success of the organization is ensured.

Leveraging technology to aid effective teamwork in the digital age:

Remote work has become an increasingly popular form of employment across various industries in today's fast-changing business world. The rise of technology has made it possible for companies to have remote teams and access global talents. To make the most of the situation, organizations must use technology to drive up productivity and deal with common challenges that arise from remote work.

1. Effective communication for seamless collaboration

Successful teamwork relies on communication, even when it is done remotely. In the absence of physical interaction, companies should provide their teams with reliable tools that will facilitate smooth collaboration. For example, video conferencing platforms are now indispensable means for holding virtual meetings because they allow real-time conversations among team members from different locations and enable screen sharing thereby ensuring connectedness. Visual cues and non-verbal gestures are possible through zoom or google meet and this also promotes instant feedback leading to effective communication among remote employees.

Moreover, there is a growing need for messaging applications alongside collaborative platforms in remote setups too. Slack, Microsoft teams, as well as basecamp among others have emerged as ideal options for quick yet efficient communication channels where team members can pass messages across or share files while working together on projects in real time without any delays whatsoever. It is also possible to create specific threads or channels within these tools so that all project-related discussions are organized well enough throughout their entire lifecycle making it easy for anyone involved in them.

2. Streamlining project management

Efficient project management is crucial if remote teams want to stay focused and achieve their goals as planned. Trello and asana are now being used by many companies seeking ways of streamlining processes within their teams by assigning tasks accordingly among other things like monitoring progress levels etc.. These two programs offer graphical designs that allow users to track individual assignments with ease by setting priorities based ontheir importance levels together with deadlines making them very useful to a busy project manager. Other features include assignment tracking, task assignment and progress update features plus notification settings making sure everyone remains on track to the end.

Additionally, document collaboration platforms such as google workspace and microsoft office 365 have played a crucial role in enhancing productivity among remote workers. By enabling simultaneous edits, version control and seamless collaboration on documents spreadsheets or presentations these tools make it easier for colleagues who might be miles apart geographically speaking to work together towards achieving shared objectives without necessarily having to send files back and forth via email. This not only reduces cases of going through file exchanges but also guarantees that every member within such teams has access to the current most updated information regarding tasks being handled at any given time.

3. Automation for enhanced efficiency

Automation tools help in increasing productivity among remote team members by getting rid of monotonous activities that eat up their time. For instance zapier, ifttt and microsoft power automate facilitate automation processes like data entry, file transfers or notifications among others thus minimizing instances where employees have to do the same tasks repeatedly allowing them to concentrate on strategic issues rather than spending resources handling non-core duties. Such improvements not only lead to better outcomes but also reduce errors improving general performance levels within the entire team.

4. Accessing a global talent pool

One major advantage associated with telecommuting involves having access to diverse talents from around the globe who can work for you remotely without necessarily being physically present at your workplace. In particular, upwork freelancer toptal are some platforms that have been created to connect employers with freelancers working from different countries allowing the hiring of specialized individuals to fill any existing gaps within organization's workforce structure. This enables businesses to collaborate across multiple fields by including industry experts possessing unique knowledge sets needed to solve complex business problems.

5. Balancing technology and a human connection

However, it is important to strike a balance between digital tools and human connection while technology plays a vital role in empowering remote teams. It should be a priority for organizations to encourage social interactions, promote a sense of camaraderie, and facilitate virtual team-building activities throughout its workforce. Through virtual events such as office gatherings for remote employees in specific regions or virtual cooking classes, social engagement can be achieved and team cohesion improved.

The way that remote teams operate and collaborate has been revolutionized by technology. By leveraging effective communication tools, streamlining project management processes, embracing automation, accessing a global talent pool, and maintaining a balance between technology and human connection; organizations can unlock the full potential of their remote teams in a digital age. In this new era of work the strategic use of technology is necessary for driving productivity, chane and transformational leadership, enhancing collaboration and achieving remarkable results regardless of geographical boundaries. Do not forget about the power of technology; you should empower your remote teams so that they can thrive in an increasingly connected and digital world.

Chapter 6

DEVELOPING PERSONAL INFLUENCE AS A TRANSFORMATIONAL LEADER

Name:

LEADERSHIP *Influence*

In its simplest form, leadership is **influence**.

Describe the relationship between leadership and influence:

Name and describe a leader who has used their influence in a *negative* way:

Name and describe a leader who has used their influence in a *positive* way:

Describe how you want to use your influence as a leader:

This vital skill plays a pivotal role in driving meaningful change and inspiring others to follow in your footsteps. In this chapter, we will delve into the significance of personal influence in transformational leadership and explore how it contributes to building trust, credibility, and respect among followers.

Personal influence is the ability to sway opinions, inspire action, and shape the thoughts and behaviors of others through one's unique qualities and characteristics. Transformational leaders who develop their personal influence possess the power to create a lasting impact within their organizations and communities.

One of the key reasons developing personal influence is important for transformational leaders is its ability to build trust among followers. Trust forms the foundation of any successful relationship, and in the context of leadership, it is crucial for motivating and inspiring others to take bold action. When leaders have developed personal influence, they establish a sense of trust that fosters loyalty, commitment, and collaboration among their followers.

Credibility is another essential element that personal influence brings to transformational leadership. Leaders who are perceived as credible are more likely to garner respect and influence others. Credibility is built upon a leader's expertise, consistency in actions, and alignment between words and deeds. By developing personal influence, transformational leaders enhance their credibility, which in turn strengthens their ability to inspire and lead others effectively.

Respect is yet another significant outcome of developing personal influence as a transformational leader. When leaders demonstrate integrity, authenticity, and empathy, they earn the respect of their followers. Respect creates an environment where ideas are valued, diverse perspectives are welcomed, and collaboration thrives. Transformational leaders who prioritize developing personal influence embody these qualities, cultivating a culture of respect that elevates both individuals and organizations.

By recognizing the importance of developing personal influence as a transformational leader, aspiring leaders can take intentional steps to hone their skills in building trust, credibility, and respect. Through self-reflection, continuous learning, and seeking feedback, leaders can identify areas for improvement and invest in personal growth. They can also learn from other influential leaders and role models who have successfully developed their personal influence.

In the following sections of this chapter, we will explore specific strategies and techniques for enhancing personal influence as a transformational leader. From enhancing leadership presence and charisma to building trust and authenticity, effective communication skills, and leveraging emotional intelligence, each aspect contributes to developing personal influence and making a lasting impact on others.

As you continue reading, remember that developing personal influence is an ongoing journey rather than a destination. It requires self-awareness, commitment, and a mindset focused on continual growth. By dedicating time and effort to developing personal influence, aspiring transformational leaders can cultivate the catalyst within themselves that ignites change, inspires greatness, and drives lasting transformation.

Enhancing leadership presence and charisma:

Developing a strong leadership presence is essential for transformational leaders to command attention, inspire others, and cultivate personal influence. A leader's presence is the culmination of their behaviors, actions, and demeanor, which can leave a lasting impact on their followers. By focusing on enhancing their leadership presence and cultivating charisma, transformational leaders can effectively engage and motivate their teams towards achieving shared goals.

One strategy for developing a strong leadership presence is to pay careful attention to body language. Nonverbal cues such as posture, gestures, and facial expressions can convey confidence, authority, and approachability. Transformational leaders should strive to maintain an open and relaxed posture, make purposeful gestures that emphasize key points, and maintain eye contact with their audience. These nonverbal signals can create a sense of trust and credibility, making it easier for followers to connect with the leader's message.

In addition to body language, vocal projection plays a crucial role in enhancing leadership presence. Transformative leaders should work on projecting their voice clearly and confidently, ensuring that their message reaches all members of their team. A strong voice demonstrates conviction and authority, leaving a lasting impression on followers. Leaders can practice vocal exercises to improve breath control, tone, and projection, allowing them to deliver impactful messages that inspire and motivate.

Storytelling is yet another powerful technique for cultivating charisma and enhancing leadership presence. Stories have the ability to captivate an audience, evoke emotions, and convey complex ideas in a relatable manner. Transformational leaders can incorporate storytelling into their communication by sharing personal anecdotes or using narratives that illustrate the importance of the team's mission and values. By weaving engaging stories into their messages, leaders can capture the attention of their followers, making them more receptive to the leader's vision and objectives.

While enhancing leadership presence and cultivating charisma are essential for transformational leaders, it is important to note that these qualities must be authentic and aligned with the leader's values and personality. A genuine and sincere approach to developing leadership presence ensures that followers perceive the leader as trustworthy and reliable.

By focusing on enhancing their leadership presence, utilizing body language, vocal projection, and storytelling techniques, transformational leaders can cultivate personal influence and inspire others to achieve greatness. Through consistent practice and commitment to authenticity, leaders can establish a strong presence that captures the hearts and minds of their followers, leading to positive change within organizations and communities.

Building trust and authenticity:

Trust and authenticity are foundational elements of developing personal influence as a transformational leader. Without trust, followers are unlikely to fully commit to a leader's vision or embrace their guidance. Authenticity, on the other hand, creates a genuine connection with others, enabling leaders to establish a sense of credibility and inspire followers to give their best.

To build trust among followers, transparency is key. Transformational leaders must be open and honest in their communications, sharing relevant information and providing clarity on their intentions and decision-making processes. Being transparent about challenges and setbacks also allows leaders to demonstrate vulnerability, which can further enhance trust.

Consistent actions are equally important in building trust. Leaders must ensure that their words align with their actions, demonstrating integrity and reliability. By consistently delivering on promises and following through on commitments, leaders establish themselves as individuals who can be trusted.

In addition to transparency and consistency, leaders can also build trust through empathy and active listening. Taking the time to understand the perspectives and concerns of followers demonstrates empathy and fosters a sense of psychological safety within the team. When followers feel heard and valued, they are more likely to trust their leader's judgment and guidance.

Authenticity goes hand in hand with trust-building. It involves being true to oneself and allowing others to see the real person behind the leadership role. Authentic leaders are genuine, displaying congruence between their values, beliefs, and actions. By embracing their unique qualities and displaying vulnerability when appropriate, leaders create a relatable persona that resonates with followers.

To cultivate authenticity, leaders should reflect on their values and purpose. By understanding what truly matters to them, they can express their passions and convictions authentically. This authenticity encourages followers to connect on a deeper level, fostering trust and loyalty.

Another strategy for building authenticity is self-reflection. Leaders should regularly assess their thoughts, feelings, and behaviors to ensure they align with their authentic self. This introspection allows leaders to identify areas for growth and improvement, leading to increased self-awareness and ultimately, more authentic leadership.

Building trust and authenticity are essential components of developing personal influence as a transformational leader. Through transparency, consistency, empathy, active listening, and embracing one's unique qualities, leaders can establish deep connections with their followers. By doing so, leaders cultivate trust and authenticity, which form the bedrock of their influence and inspire meaningful change within their organizations and communities.

Developing personal influence as a transformational leader: effective communication skills:

Communication lies at the heart of effective leadership, playing a crucial role in influencing others and driving transformative change. In this section, we will delve into the importance of effective communication skills for transformational leaders, providing valuable guidance on improving verbal and nonverbal communication, active listening, and empathy.

Verbal communication is a vital tool for transformational leaders to convey their vision, inspire others, and motivate action. It is essential to articulate ideas clearly, using concise and compelling language that resonates with followers. Transformational leaders should strive for clarity, avoiding jargon or overly complex terminology that might alienate or confuse their audience. By engaging in open, honest, and transparent communication, leaders can foster trust and create an environment where ideas can flourish.

Nonverbal communication also plays a significant role in conveying messages and building personal influence. Leaders must understand the impact of their body language, facial expressions, and gestures, ensuring they align with the desired message. Maintaining eye contact, adopting an open posture, and using appropriate hand movements can enhance a leader's credibility and engage their audience.

Active listening is a skill that distinguishes exceptional leaders from ordinary ones. Transformational leaders prioritize listening to their followers genuinely. They take the time to understand their concerns, needs, and aspirations actively. Through active listening, leaders demonstrate empathy and build trust with their followers. They validate others' perspectives, allowing for collaboration and open dialogue.

Empathy is a critical aspect of effective communication for transformational leaders. By putting themselves in the shoes of their followers and striving to understand their emotions and experiences, leaders can forge deeper connections. Empathetic leaders acknowledge the feelings of others and respond with compassion and understanding. This fosters a sense of psychological safety within the organization, enabling individuals to bring their authentic selves to work.

Effective communication skills are essential tools in developing personal influence as a transformational leader. By improving verbal and nonverbal communication, practicing active listening, and cultivating empathy, leaders can create meaningful connections, inspire others, and drive lasting change.

Next, we will explore the role of emotional intelligence in developing personal influence as a transformational leader.

Developing personal influence as a transformational leader: leveraging emotional intelligence:

In the quest to develop personal influence as a transformational leader, one cannot overlook the vital role of emotional intelligence. Emotional intelligence refers to the ability to recognize and understand one's own emotions and the emotions of others, and to use this understanding to guide thinking and behavior. It is an essential tool in building influential connections with followers and inspiring them to take positive action.

Self-awareness is the foundation upon which emotional intelligence is built. As a transformational leader, cultivating self-awareness involves a deep understanding of one's own emotions, strengths, weaknesses, values, and triggers. This self-reflection enables leaders to understand how their emotions impact their behavior and decision-making, allowing them to make conscious choices in how they lead.

Self-regulation is the next crucial aspect of leveraging emotional intelligence. It involves managing one's own emotions in difficult situations and responding appropriately rather than reacting impulsively. Transformational leaders who can regulate their emotions create an environment of stability and calmness, fostering trust and confidence among their followers.

Empathy plays a vital role in developing personal influence as well. Transformational leaders with high levels of empathy possess the ability to understand and share the feelings of others. By putting themselves in the shoes of their followers, leaders can better relate to their experiences, needs, and aspirations. This empathetic understanding allows leaders to connect on a deeper level, creating trust and loyalty.

Relationship management is the final component of leveraging emotional intelligence to develop personal influence. Effective relationship management involves building strong connections with followers based on trust, respect, and open communication. Transformational leaders who excel in relationship management create an environment where individuals feel valued, heard, and supported. They invest time in getting to know their followers personally, recognizing their strengths, and providing opportunities for growth.

By leveraging emotional intelligence, transformational leaders can forge influential connections that inspire followers to reach their full potential. The ability to understand and manage emotions, demonstrate empathy, and foster positive relationships is what sets transformational leaders apart. In a world where emotional intelligence is often undervalued, those leaders who embrace it will not only develop personal influence but also create a lasting impact on their organizations and communities.

Aspiring transformational leaders must prioritize the development of their emotional intelligence alongside other key leadership skills. By doing so, they will cultivate the personal influence necessary to inspire lasting change and become catalysts for transformation.

Your roadmap to increasing your influence at work:

One of the most invaluable assets a leader can have is personal influence. Being able to motivate, inspire and guide others towards a common goal is key to being successful. Yet building up and increasing personal influence is not always simple. It takes trust, effective communication skills along with deep understanding of others. In this article we will look at practical ways on how you can enhance your personal influence as an effective leader.

1. Building trust through relationships:

Trust is the basis of personal influence. It is the confidence that others have in your character, competence and dependability. Without trust it becomes difficult to gain influence over other people. To foster trust start by creating genuine relationships with members of your team or colleagues. Take time to know their goals, aspirations as well as challenges they face in life. Engage in open conversations where both parties get heard while actively listening out for concerns from either side then show empathy towards them. By investing in relationship building you create a strong foundation upon which trust will support your leadership influence.

"don't fall into the trap of thinking leadership of any kind is a thing you do to others. Leadership is at its core a relationship in which one person trusts the other enough to follow them because they want to go where they're being led of their own accord."

2. Understanding others' goals and needs:

To successfully influence others it is important to understand what their goals are and what they need. Have meaningful conversations with the members of your team or colleagues so that you can learn about their objectives for example ask them what are you trying to achieve? Use techniques like "five whys" technique that helps dig deeper into underlying motivations behind someone's behavior or decisions etc.. When you understand how success looks like from their point hence providing necessary support together with guidance when necessary this common understanding builds trust making you even more influential as a leader

"focus on learning what other people or teams are trying to accomplish by talking to them. Run the five whys* with them -- work from their wants to their needs until you get to something specific."

* "the five whys" is a problem-solving technique that allows people to find out the root cause of problems by asking "why" repeatedly until they get to the main reason. In teamwork, it enables you to identify and overcome the obstacles that hinder effective collaboration.

Surface-level issue:

Find a specific issue or challenge relating to teamwork.

First "why":

Ask how the problem occurred which helps in identifying its immediate cause.

Second "why":

This question is asked again for the previous response. This will let you know more about why an immediate cause occurs in the first instance.

Third "why":

Repeat this process for the earlier answer. Ask why and you will discover more about the underlying reasons behind the causation.

Fourth and fifth "why":

Keep on asking why until you reach the fifth one. The fifth response point will be your root cause.

In applying "the five whys" to teamwork, it is important to have open communication, willingness to explore deeper issues, as well as a collaborative effort aimed at addressing the root causes and implementing effective solutions conducive to transformation and change.

3. Collaboration and shared goals:

Collaboration is a powerful tool for increasing personal influence. When you work together with others towards a common goal, you create a sense of unity and purpose. Identify shared objectives then find ways in which your goals align with those of team members or colleagues. This approach allows everyone involved to feel ownership making it easy to influence and inspire other people. While working towards these set targets consistently communicate them as well as reinforce the idea that teamwork pays off for all parties involved.

"share what you're trying to accomplish and venn diagram your goals and their goals and work out what's shared and do what you can to support it and invite them to do the same."

4. Solving problems together:

"leaders have an opportunity to solve both small and big problems for others by not simply jumping in and doing something for them, but by working with them through the challenges as a team."

5. Leading by example:

To increase personal influence, it is important that you lead by example. Your actions and behaviors will set the atmosphere for those around you. Show others what you expect from them in terms of qualities and values including integrity, accountability, resilience among others. Be a role model to your team members or colleagues showing them what it takes to be a good leader. By consistently exhibiting the characteristics you want others to possess, they get inspired to copy your behavior thereby increasing their trust and respect towards you.

"in the end, you'll have gained a lot of trust and shown you can help people find a way forward just like a leader."

6. Effective communication skills:

Any leader who wants to increase their personal influence must have effective communication skills. Practice active listening so that you understand where they are coming from. In your communication use their language and context so that you can establish connection as well as foster understanding. Remember your tone, body language, choice of words among other things while delivering your message as they can either positively or negatively impact on its reception. Through honing communication skills, one is able to effectively pass on their ideas to others thus inspiring them thereby enhancing their influence as leaders.

"work on your communication skills including both verbal and non-verbal communication; such factors like; tone, language used, body language should be considered when building up image."

7. Actively market yourself:

It's saliently important for one to actively market himself or herself if he/she wants more influence in life. Use various platforms like social media sites, speaking engagements at public forums, or networking events where you can showcase expertise achievements etcetera craft an appealing personal brand which will enable you to stand out among many others having similar offers. Through strategic positioning yourself as an industry expert/thought leader, people will start watching, believing and eventually follow in your steps.

"to have greater influence in their career candidates need to actively market themselves. This includes having what's conveyed in the résumé, online job profiles and interviews work in concert to match what recruiters, managers, and companies are looking for."

8. Continual self-development:

In order to increase one's personal influence as a leader; personal growth and self-development are very important. Continue seeking opportunities that help you expand your knowledge, skills or even perspectives. Seek relevant training; attend conferences etc.. So that you can keep on learning. By investing in your own development, you show commitment towards growth as well as improvement which also inspires others to do the same. As you become knowledgeable and capable of doing things, your influence level naturally goes up because people believe in your abilities thereby following whatever instructions given by you easily.

Cultivate empathy by putting yourself in others' shoes and seek to understand their perspectives and feelings. Show genuine care and concern for the well-being of your team members or colleagues. Emotional intelligence allows you to recognize and manage your own emotions and empathize with others' emotions. By fostering empathy and emotional intelligence, you can create a supportive and inclusive environment that enhances your influence as a leader.

Freely share your knowledge, talents, and resources with others. Show a genuine interest in their success and well-being. By being generous and authentic, you create a positive cycle of recognition and contribution that strengthens your influence. When others see your commitment and care, they will be more inclined to listen to your ideas and follow your lead.

Integrity is necessary for personal influence and sets a good example which other individuals should then emulate. Consistently act in alignment with your values and ethical principles as well as being transparent & honest in all of your interactions then people will respect/trust you as their leader, this is especially true during periods of transformation and change.

Chapter 7

OVERCOMING CHALLENGES AND ADVERSITY: LESSONS FROM INFLUENTIAL LEADERS

The Adkar change model:

Adkar change model is a widely used change management approach that offers a roadmap for navigating organizational change effectively. It consists of five key stages as follows:

Awareness:

Increase individual's awareness about the change and make sure they comprehend why it is necessary.

Desire:

Create a desire to embrace change. This includes creating a positive attitude or motivation among stakeholders.

Knowledge:

Give individuals the knowledge and information they need on the changes so that they understand the specifics and implications.

Ability:

Provide individuals with skills and tools needed for successful implementation of the change. In this phase, emphasis is put on practical application.

Reinforcement:

Implement reinforcement measures to sustain the change. This involves appreciating and rewarding people who adopt change to ensure its continued existence in an organization.

The Adkar model helps in identifying potential barriers to change in terms of individual roles, thus facilitating smoother transition processes. When applied well, it enhances organizational adaptability, while minimizing resistance towards change.

ADKAR Change Model

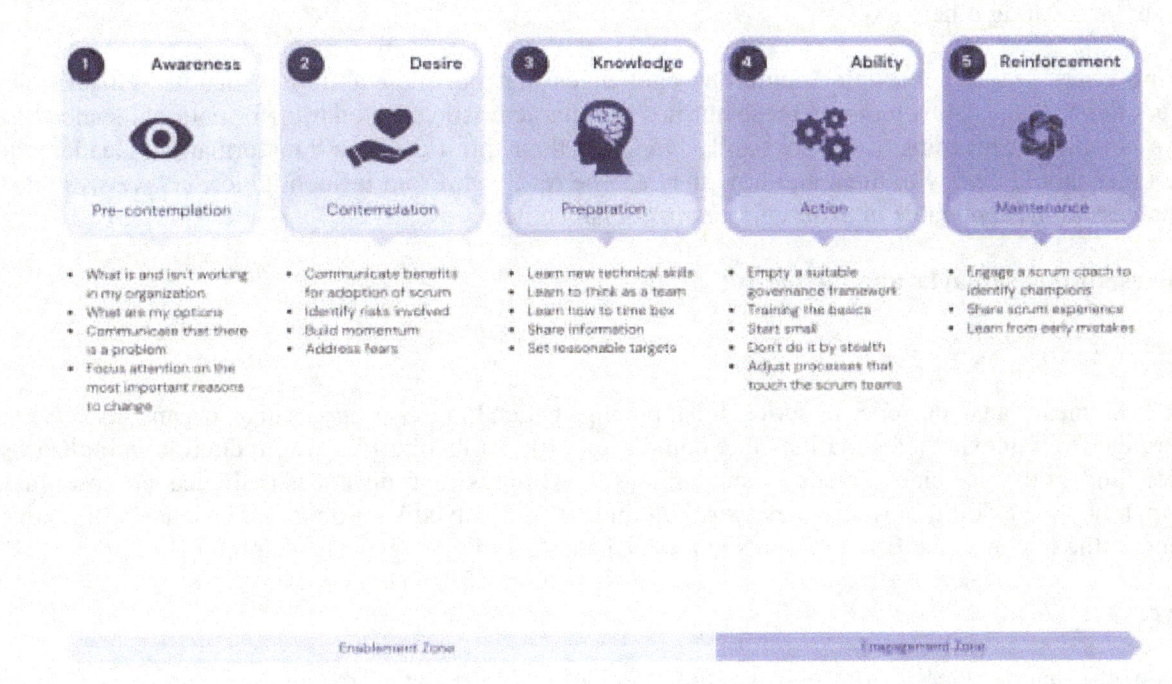

The significance of resilience:

Resilient leaders know that in order to overcome inevitable challenges and adversity in leadership it is important to develop and maintain resilient mindsets and behaviours. This means being able to bounce back from setbacks, adapt to change, and stay strong when things get tough. Such a trait helps leaders overcome obstacles as well as persuade others to do the same.

Leaders who are resilient have a deep understanding of their own strengths and weaknesses, which enables them to navigate through difficult situations effectively. They are also optimistic about life and persistent towards achieving goals; they perceive obstacles as opportunities for growth rather than insurmountable barriers. By being positive thinkers at all times, they can inspire themselves and their groups even during trying moments.

Furthermore, influential leaders recognize how self-care and stress management contribute towards resilience building. They put themselves first in terms of physical health, mental wellness, and emotional stability because taking care of oneself allows an individual to better deal with tough situations. This may involve practicing mindfulness techniques or seeking help from mentors/peers or engaging in activities that promote relaxation.

In addition, influential leaders also embrace failure as part of the learning process towards developing resilient mindsets and behaviors within the context of leadership. They understand that failing is inevitable therefore gaining valuable lessons which can be used to drive personal growth as well as organizational development. Instead of getting discouraged by failures; they take them as stepping stones towards success. Resilient leaders become more ready for future challenges through learning from mistakes thus adjusting strategies appropriately.

By drawing inspiration from real-life examples where influential leaders have demonstrated resilience amidst adversity, this chapter highlights its essential role in effective leadership. Their stories will enable readers to gain insights into how these individuals built up their courage despite the adversities faced while maintaining focus on their goals till triumphing over all odds. With similar mindset and behavior patterns; aspiring transformational leaders can enhance their capacity to overcome difficulties thereby motivating others too.

During crisis, leaders encounter numerous challenges that put their ability to handle setbacks and adversities to the test. Overcoming these hurdles is a characteristic of good transformational leadership. Let's examine the meaning of setbacks and adversities, their significance in transformational leadership, when one should deal with them and how they can be resolved. From influential leaders we will learn valuable lessons applicable in different organizational contexts.

Understanding setbacks and adversity:

Setbacks:

A setback means an occurrence or series of happenings which hinders progress in an organization. They can range from unexpected situations like demolition of historical buildings or reduction in budget by major funders to false claims made by media houses. At times such instances make leaders lose track of what they were doing or where they were heading; even if solved later on its effects may still remain either on the image of the firm or doubts among stakeholders in the leader's vision.

Adversity:

On the other hand; adversity is a persistent unfavorable condition that makes it hard for any organization to move forward. It might include lack of resources, community opposition or ongoing difficulties in reaching intended clients among others. While setbacks are usually single occurrences; adversity lasts for a longer duration thus forcing leaders to navigate multiple challenges and changes in circumstance.

The importance of overcoming setbacks and adversity:

The ability to overcome setbacks and adversity is crucial for several reasons:

1. Sustaining forward momentum:

Organizations need to learn and adapt continuously to remain healthy. Setbacks and adversity, if not properly addressed, can halt progress and even push an organization backward. Regardless of the difficulties faced, transformational leaders must maintain a focus on their vision and goals and strive to improve their work and operations daily.

2. Fostering resilience and optimism:

In challenging times it is easy to succumb to discouragement and despair. Effective and transformational leaders have the responsibility of inspiring and maintaining high morale among their staff and volunteers. By demonstrating resilience and optimism, leaders can instill a sense of hope reminding everyone that troubles will eventually pass, and things will improve.

3. Building trust and reputation:

Overcoming setbacks and adversity can enhance an organization's reputation in two ways. Firstly, by maintaining high performance standards, leaders establish themselves as effective and reliable. Secondly, successfully navigating through difficult situations demonstrates the organization's competence, dedication, and ability to serve the community even in challenging times.

4. Learning and growth:

Setbacks and adversity provide valuable opportunities for learning and growth. By analyzing these challenges' causes as well as consequences; leaders can identify areas for improvement while developing strategies that ensure such situations do not arise again in future times ahead for instance; embracing setbacks as learning experiences which may lead to enhanced knowledge base(s) among others such skill-set development within organizations over long term periods of time.

5. Personal and leadership development:

Overcoming setbacks is a character-building experience for leaders when faced with an obstacle in their respective sectors or industries they tend not just merely giving up on it but rather find out what went wrong, what did i miss? Each challenge provides them an opportunity for personal growth and realization of their leadership potential.

6. Maintaining faith in leadership:

How leaders handle setbacks and adversity significantly impacts the organization's faith in their leadership. By effectively managing difficult situations, leaders build trust and credibility among their team members, ensuring continued support and commitment during challenging times.

7. Staying focused on the mission:

During setbacks and adversity it is important to stay focused on the mission of an organization.this means continuing to serve its intended beneficiaries despite any challenges that may be encountered along this path. By keeping this at the forefront, leaders can inspire their team members to persevere and work towards meaningful change even when faced with adversity.

Working towards overcoming setbacks and adversity:

Timing plays a crucial role in addressing setbacks and adversity. Leaders must adapt their approaches based on the nature of the challenge they face.

Overcoming setbacks:

When encountering a setback, immediate action is often necessary. Leaders should aim to:

Stay calm: in order for clear decision-making, a calm confident demeanor should be maintained which reassures people within the organization as well as allows them make sound choices especially during periods when everybody else's panicked.

Communicate: keeping everyone informed about the setback and subsequent plan of action is vital because it prevents rumors from spreading while maintaining trust between individuals involved even though some might opt against sharing such information here we need transparency otherwise there'll be confusion leading to mistrust.

Take action: demonstrate proactivity through taking appropriate steps aimed at addressing a given challenge albeit not necessarily being an instant solution, this shows determination and commitment moving forward irrespective of circumstances and coalesces faith in the leader's vision.

Learn from experience: reflecting upon setbacks gives valuable insights useful future decision-making processes which may further prevent recurrence similar cases happening again elsewhere for instance; by reflecting upon this experience.

Overcoming adversity:

In face of adversity, leaders should adopt a more long-term approach emphasizing perseverance and steady progress. Key strategies include:

Stay calm and steadfast: consistently projecting a calm composed demeanor reassures colleagues and helps maintain a sense of stability in the chaos of crisis.

Overcoming setbacks and adversity in transformational leadership:

Effective transformational leadership involves overcoming setbacks and adversity. It therefore requires resilience, optimism-inspiring leaders, and navigators who are undeterred by challenges. We can strengthen our own leadership skills and guide organizations towards success by learning from influential leaders and applying their lessons even during the most challenging times. Remember, setbacks and adversity are not roadblocks; they are opportunities for growth and transformation. Embrace them, learn from them, and lead your organization towards a brighter future.

Communicate and provide guidance: in order to help the organization navigate through the challenges presented by adversity, open communication is necessary alongside clear guidance.

Take appropriate action: when faced with an adverse situation, it is important for leaders to take measured and strategic action considering long-term goals as well as the ability of the organization to adapt.

Encourage learning and growth: within the organization, viewing adversity as an opportunity for learning fosters a growth mindset that supports continuous improvement.

Seek support: leaders should not hesitate to seek support from trusted individuals who can provide guidance on how to navigate through difficult times.

Examples from influential leaders:

Throughout history there have been many influential leaders who have demonstrated the ability to overcome setbacks and adversity. By studying their experiences, we can gain valuable insights that will enable us to apply these principles within our own leadership journeys. Below are a few examples:

Example 1: warren Bennis:

Having served as a young lieutenant in world war ii, warren Bennis drew lessons from his experiences that led him into becoming one of today's most renowned leadership experts. He learned leadership goes beyond just personal actions as it impacts others' lives profoundly too. This led to him promoting a leadership style that actively engaged others in his vision, communicating effectively while maintaining strong values based on integrity, empathy and trust.

Example 2: franklin d. Roosevelt:

In America's history, franklin d. Roosevelt was the thirty-second president tasked with leading America through the great depression in the 1930's. During this period, his ability to remain calm, communicate effectively, and take decisive action restored faith in government and initiated 'the new deal' aimed at mitigating the effects of the most serious economic crisis of our times, and helping massively reduce unemployment that was otherwise out of control.

Example 3: Nelson Mandela:

Throughout his life nelson Mandela faced numerous setbacks and adversity even after becoming south Africa's iconic anti-apartheid leader as well as former president. Despite being imprisoned for 27 years, he still had a vision of a democratic south Africa that finally became true, making him a symbol of resilience and forgiveness. His ability to stay focused on the mission while inspiring others provides a powerful example of leadership amidst adversity.

For an effective transformational leader, overcoming setbacks and adversity is a crucial aspect of their ability to be a catalyst for change. Remember that setbacks and adversity are not roadblocks but rather opportunities for growth and transformation. Embrace them, learn from them and lead your organization towards a brighter future.

When faced with difficult situations, effectively leaders show how good they are at solving problems by using practical techniques and strategies. They know that effective problem-solving is a process which involves more than simply identifying the issue in question. They find innovative solutions inside complex problems often through highly developed emotional intelligence.

One part of emotional intelligence is self-awareness which means recognizing and understanding one's own emotions, strengths, weaknesses, and triggers. Influential leaders with high levels of self-awareness can control their feelings better hence respond calmly even when confronted by tough situations. They are aware of how they feel emotionally and can effectively regulate their behaviors so as to avoid being engulfed by negativity.

In addition to self-awareness, influential leaders also exhibit empathy towards their team members as well as other colleagues. This means that they have the ability to put themselves in others' shoes thus leading to trust, connection, and collaboration during a crisis. Through empathy, transformative leaders establish an atmosphere where individuals are comprehended for who they are, what they do and feel inspired enough to walk together over hurdles.

Moreover, emotionally intelligent leaders excel in managing relationships and communicating effectively even when things become tough for them. They possess skills for noting emotional changes in group members and responding appropriately either through guidance or offering moral support among others. By acknowledging their team's feelings as well as validating them out loud; influential managers create a sense of unity, endurance and collective power necessary for overcoming challenges.

Chapter 8

THE EVOLUTION OF TRANSFORMATIONAL LEADERSHIP THEORIES AND MODELS:

Our view of the transformational leadership style and role has been influenced by the rich history of leadership models and management theory. In this chapter we will first provide an overview of the conditions in which the theories of transformational leadership developed and also look at some key personalities who have helped shape our understanding of this powerful way to lead.

During the 1970s, transformational leadership theories emerged from more traditional management theories as scholars began to question the traditional notion of leader as transactional and only interested in rewards and punishments. One of the early pioneers in this field was James MacGregor burns who introduced a new concept called "transformational leadership" in his book called leadership published in 1978 which is considered a classic work on the subject. According to him, leaders are not just those who give people rewards for their compliance but go beyond that by inspiring them through personal power such as charisma, vision etc so as to achieve extraordinary results from them.

Later researchers built upon burns' work by further developing and refining the concept of transformational leadership. Similarly Bernard m. Bass, another well-known authority on leadership extended what had been said by burns while bringing about his full range leadership model. Transformational, transactional, and laissez-faire (passive-avoidant) are the three main management styles identified by bass under his model which we will discuss later in this chapter.

Bruce j Avolio and Bernard m bass later developed the multifactor leadership questionnaire (MLQ) which is another influential framework model within transformational leadership. It measures different aspects of leadership including idealized influence; intellectual stimulation; individualized consideration among other aspects related specifically with transformational leadership. This tool has been widely used for measuring transformative behaviors among various groups working under different organizations.

In MLQ form 5x-short there are various Likert scale rated items designed to assess leadership the degree of the various leadership styles. Here are some sample items taken from MLQ.

"i try to make my team members understand importance their tasks showing how these fit into bigger picture."

"i provide my team members with feedback on how well they are doing."

"i don't take charge of decision making in my group; i let them make their own choices."

These questions illustrate diversity in mlq, capturing both transformational, transactional as well as passive-avoidant types of leadership styles. Respondents rate their agreement or disagreement with such statements to determine their leadership preferences and behaviors. The mlq is administered in both self and rater forms for comprehensive assessment where one learns about oneself while others learn about him or her as leader.

However there have been some criticisms leveled against this approach despite several advances made in the theory of transformational leadership. Scholars have noted that failure to identify specific defining criteria within theoretical constructs makes it difficult for consistent measurements and replication purposes hence limiting its usefulness. Additionally, critics argue that by focusing only on positive aspects associated with transformational leaders we may overlook negative consequences that could result from extreme charismatic personalities, sometimes known as the adolf hitler paradox.

Researchers have made advancements in various areas to address these critiques and refine our understanding of transformational leadership. They have explored the role of contextual factors and follower characteristics in influencing the effectiveness of transformational leadership. Furthermore, researchers have now delved into the psychological theories of charisma. Max weber came up with charismatic as a term which describes exceptional qualities that leaders possess to inspire loyalty and devotion among their followers. Charismatic transformational leaders use charm, persuasion, and magnetic personality to captivate and mobilize others.

Subsequent researchers built upon these early theories to further develop the concept of modern transformational leadership. They introduced theoretical frameworks and models that expanded our understanding of this leadership style. One notable framework already touched on is bernard bass's full range leadership model, which categorizes leadership behaviors into three main styles: transformational, transactional, and laissez-faire.

Bass's model emphasizes the transformative nature of transformational leadership thus highlighting its ability to inspire followers beyond their self-interest towards a collective vision. It also recognizes transactional leadership behaviors such as rewards and punishments as important tools towards achieving organizational goals (burns 1978). Furthermore, this model acknowledges the negative impact associated with laissez-faire leadership where leaders fail to provide guidance or support for their followers while abdicating their responsibilities within organizations.

As the field of transformational leadership continues to evolve, it is important to recognize the significant contributions of early theories and foundational concepts. These theories paved the way for subsequent developments helping us understand how much power lies in good leadership for instance (bass & Riggio 2006).

The evolution of transformational leadership theories and models has seen the emergence of various prominent theoretical frameworks and models that have greatly contributed to our understanding of this leadership style. These frameworks provide valuable insights into the key components and characteristics of transformational leadership which guide leaders in their quest for inspiring positive change.

Another influential model/framework we'll discuss in more detail is Avolio and yammering's multifactor leadership questionnaire (MLQ), which measures various aspects of transformational leadership including idealized influence, inspirational motivation, intellectual stimulation, and individualized consideration. The MLQ provides a comprehensive assessment of transformational leadership behaviors thereby enabling researchers and practitioners to better understand and measure the impact of transformational leaders. It is an important tool in analyzing transformational leadership and monitoring their effect on organizational change.

The multi-factor leadership questionnaire assesses nine different factors within the transformational leadership domain including idealized influence (attributed and behavior), inspirational motivation, intellectual stimulation, and individualized consideration. By evaluating these factors, the mlq provides a comprehensive understanding of a leader's transformational behaviors as well as their impact on followers.

This questionnaire is a useful tool helping leaders identify areas where they can enhance their transformational behaviors while leveraging their influence towards driving lasting change. By incorporating elements from these models into their leadership practice leaders can make a more significant impact on their organizations and communities they represent.

Researchers are continuously investigating new trends and new directions as the field of transformational leadership continue to evolve. Some emerging areas of focus include looking at the intersection between transformational leadership styles and other management styles like authentic and ethical ones to reveal synergies that can be harnessed or integrated. There are also some scholars who are studying how transformational leadership applies in different contexts such as cross-cultural settings or virtual teams so that they can know how this style comes about and changes within various environments.

By keeping up with these recent trends as well as future directions in research on transformational leadership, leaders can continually fine-tune their approach towards leading people in order to cater for changing demands in their organizations.

Critiques and advancements in transformational leadership theories:

Although early theories laid down its foundation, critics argued that these approaches were not without limitations. As researchers delved more into this concept, progress was made by responding to criticisms while deepening our knowledge about it.

One of the main critiques directed towards initial theories was their lack of clarity regarding what constituted such a form of management practice and how it could be measured. It was said that indeed defining what actually constitutes transformational leadership within an organization is not easy because there are no tangible tools which one may use for assessing its effectiveness, in part this was why the MLQ was developed. Consequently, subsequent researchers came up with more specific frameworks and models whereby behaviors associated with transformative leaders become apparent, it is important to know that transformational leadership is as much an art as a science and it is constantly evolving and changing, just like a true catalyst for change.

Also, attempts have been made to examine how culture and context affect the effectiveness of transformative leadership. Some researchers recognized that what may be considered as transformative or empathetic in one culture or context might not necessarily translate exactly into another. By recognizing these nuances, progress has been made towards understanding how cultural and contextual factors shape its manifestation and impact.

Another area of focus in contemporary transformational leadership research pertains to its applicability in different contexts. Transformational leadership was early researched under corporate settings, but now scholars are examining how it works in non-profit organizations, education, health and government. This broadening of studies across various sectors allows people to understand better how this kind of leadership can be tailored or adapted for use in different environments. For the purpose of this book we take a general viewpoint tackling transactional leadership in such a way it can be applied to any setting.

Furthermore, it has to be said, there is growing interest in exploring the role of transformational leadership in addressing contemporary challenges and societal issues. The researchers are studying how transformative leaders can lead through crises effectively; support sustainable practices; promote social justice, climate action and equity within their organizations and communities. This shift towards examining the broader impact of transformational leadership aligns with the increasing recognition that leaders have a responsibility to address complex societal problems beyond their immediate organizational contexts.

Looking ahead, what does the future holds for research on transformational? One possible direction is integration technology artificial intelligence into study transformational leadership. With advances in data analytics and machine learning researchers will have deeper insights about behaviors, traits associated with change catalysts as well as effectiveness assessment measures adopted by them. Moreover, exploring how technology can augment or support transformational leadership practices may open up new avenues for leadership development and organizational transformation as well as deeper ethical concerns.

Staying current with the latest trends and future directions in transformational leadership research is essential for leaders seeking to cultivate their own catalysts for lasting change. By understanding the intersection between the transformational style and others and exploring the style's applicability across diverse domains and embracing emerging areas of study aspiring transformational leaders can continuously refine their practices and become true catalysts for change within their organizations.

Chapter 9

CHARISMATIC LEADERSHIP: HARNESSING CHARISMA FOR POSITIVE CHANGE

Charismatic leaders typically have exceptional influence on people's lives. As we delve into this section, we will define charismatic leadership and explore its significance in driving positive change within organizations and communities.

Charismatic leaders possess a unique set of traits and behaviors that set them apart from others. They have the innate ability to inspire and motivate their followers, leaving a lasting impression that compels others to take action. It is through their magnetic personality, exceptional communication skills, and powerful presence that charismatic leaders create a strong connection with those they lead.

One of the defining characteristics of charismatic leaders is their ability to articulate a compelling vision that resonates with others. They paint a vivid picture of the future, instilling hope and inspiring their teams to work towards shared goals. Their visionary mindset enables them to see opportunities where others may only see challenges, uplifting and empowering their followers to overcome obstacles.

Charismatic leaders are also effective communicators. They have excellent listening skills, enabling them to understand their followers' wants, hopes and fears. By being attentive and responsive, they build strong relationships based on mutual respect and understanding. Moreover, charismatic leaders can use persuasive language and storytelling techniques to convey their messages with impact, evoking emotions that resonate deeply with others.

Charismatic leadership has many benefits; however, charismatic leaders must find a balance between these qualities and other important ones. They should remain humble and authentic so as not to fall into the traps of excessive dependence on their charisma. By grounding themselves in humility and authenticity, charismatic leaders can maintain their credibility, trustworthiness, and long-term effectiveness.

Let's look more deeply into how charisma inspires others & come up with practical strategies that will help you develop into a leader who possesses such qualities. Through understanding what charismatic leadership is about including its role within transformational leadership then we could be able to tap into the power of charisma so as to inspire meaningful changes within our teams or even our communities at large.

The power of charisma in inspiring others:

There are several key ways through which charisma impacts other people specifically when it comes to motivating them towards taking up action towards embracing change. Normally these kinds of individuals usually captivate the audience by painting out vivid pictures aand stories about what tomorrow holds while introducing purpose and direction that otherwise might be lacking among their followers as well as being effective communicators.

Moreover, charisma plays a critical role in regard to building trust & credibility between followers & their leaders. These charismatic individuals are usually confident, warm hearted and genuine; thus creating an open atmosphere where each and every person feels free to share his/her thoughts with others. Once someone sees that his/her leader is charismatic then automatically such a person would be more likely to trust him/her more because psychologically they are signalling there are higher chances that such an individual has good intentions, numerous studies show we are more likely to trust a charismatic leader. This trust is very important when it comes to establishing strong relationships within the team while at the same time ensuring that there is unity among workers so as to promote productivity and drive change.

Apart from inspiring actions & fostering trust, charisma also possesses the ability of attracting others towards oneself like a magnet. Charismatic leaders have always been known for their ability to draw people in making them feel valued, seen and heard.

However, that said, charismatic leaders should balance their charisma with humility and authenticity. Charisma can be helpful in leadership but it should not overshadow being real and humble. Leaders should not forget that charisma is not enough to hold long-term influence and impact. For leaders to cause lasting changes, they must mix charisma with authentic actions and genuine care for others; this way, they will keep their teams' trust and loyalty.

In summary, charisma has a huge role to play when it comes to motivating others as well as ensuring positive change within organizations. Charisma's impact is seen through its ability to motivate people, create trustworthiness, credibility and establish a sense of loyalty. However, there is a need for leaders to balance between charisma, humility and authenticity in order to achieve sustainable influence as well as long term success. Through the power of charisma, leaders can inspire greatness, catalyze catalysts and uncover the forces behind transformational leadership.

Cultivating charismatic qualities as a leader:

Charisma does not come naturally; it is something you have learned how to do over time. Transformational leaders use charisma which often carries along magnetic charm and influence that inspires others driving positive change. We will discuss various ways of developing this charm by defining the key characteristics of charismatic persons and suggesting practical steps for boosting your personal charisma.

1. Self-awareness: self-awareness makes one develop charisma by allowing someone to understand their own feelings and emotions this makes projecting authenticity easier as well as allowing the leader to practice on areas of deficiency. Take time to reflect on your values, motivations and aspirations because they will help you understand yourself better thus aligning your goals & actions based on defined purpose making your presence more real rather than fake.
2. Confidence: confidence is a fundamental element of an attractive demeanor. It involves believing in your own competence, judgments, and ideas. To build confidence, recognize your achievements and strengths. Surround yourself with positive people and seek feedback to help you see areas where you can improve. Learn to be assertive in expressing your thoughts and opinions while being open minded.
3. Strong communication skills: any charismatic leader needs effective communication skills. Work on expressing your ideas straightforwardly. Look at the way you use your body when talking or walking or what expression you have on your face as well as tone of voice. Listen actively to others so they feel important and understood by you thus making them believe in themselves more. You will become better at connecting with other people if you develop good communication skills.
4. Authenticity: charisma is built on being real with oneself; therefore, accept who you are as a leader and strive to show it whenever interacting with anyone else around you. Don't pretend or act like someone else because this won't work for long periods, insecure individuals cannot inspire others since they don't feel comfortable enough within their own skins while leaders who embrace their weaknesses attract followers quite easily due to their perceived vulnerability.
5. Emotional intelligence: emotionally intelligent charismatic leaders understand how their feelings impact upon those around them while also empathizing with people's situations too high levels of emotional intelligence make a person capable of understanding and managing his/her emotions as well as showing compassion towards others.

6. Positive mindset: even during difficult moments, charismatic leaders still emanate positive vibes. Adopting this perspective will enable you to inspire those who may be feeling down or discouraged thereby fostering an environment conducive for creativity as well as enabling people to overcome challenges through resilience and growth.

7. Continuous learning: never stop learning even if one has become a leader already; therefore, always strive to improve yourself through education and personal development. Find ways to expand your knowledge base; take advantage of new opportunities that come your way; keep yourself informed of the latest trends occurring across various industries and do not reject constructive criticism.

Remember that developing charisma is an ongoing process. It requires consistent self-reflection, practice, and a genuine desire to connect with and inspire others. As you cultivate these charismatic qualities within yourself, you will be better equipped to harness the power of charisma for positive change in your organization and community.

Leveraging charisma to drive positive change:

Charismatic leaders have a unique ability to get others excited about new ideas and motivate them into action as well due their magnetism which attracts people towards them together with compelling communication skills that they use convey messages leading shared visions among teams finally let us discuss some strategies on how we can apply this quality in driving good changes both within our organizations and communities at large around us right now today;

In order to communicate their vision effectively, charismatic leaders must be able to tell stories powerfully. Storytelling is a powerful way to evoke human emotions and establish a deep connection between the leader and his or her followers. Through personal anecdotes, examples, or success stories, these leaders can make the audience understand what they want to achieve in real terms. This emotional engagement builds trust, involvement, and mutual commitment to positive change.

Moreover, charismatic leaders know how to motivate teams towards common goals. They realize that when people have an emotional stake in change, they are more likely to accept it. By inspiring people through their words and actions, these leaders use their ability to move masses. They create urgency and excitement by pointing out the potential rewards and benefits of actively participating in the change processes.

Additionally, charismatic leaders are good at building strong relationships with members of their team. They take time out of their busy schedules just so that they can connect with individuals on a personal level displaying empathy as well as active listening skills among others showing respect too. Charismatic leadership entails showing care and concern for the overall well-being of followers thereby establishing trust and loyalty leading to motivation where every person feels like giving out his or her best towards achieving shared goals.

Leveraging charisma as an agent for driving positive change requires effective communication of a compelling vision coupled with motivating teams toward common objectives. Charismatic leaders develop clarity by crafting a vision that inspires change; they also employ storytelling techniques which are powerful tools used in conveying messages vividly making them memorable after hearing them once only; finally developing strong relationships between one's team members such as being open-minded when dealing with others' opinions while still maintaining accountability levels within teams (bass & Riggio 2012). With their unique ability to ignite passion and enthusiasm, charismatic leaders create a ripple effect driving lasting positive changes within organizations and communities as whole.

Charismatic leadership: harnessing charisma for positive change: balancing charisma with humility and authenticity

As we delve deeper into the concept of charismatic leadership, it is crucial to explore the delicate balance between charisma and two essential qualities: humility and authenticity. Although charisma has been known to inspire and motivate, its effectiveness can dwindle if not tempered with these complementary traits.

Maintaining authenticity is vital for building trust and credibility as a charismatic leader. When followers perceive a leader as genuine and true to themselves, they are more likely to trust their vision and willingly contribute towards achieving shared goals. This fosters an environment of openness where honesty prevails thus making it easier for people to relate well with each other through effective communication methods (bass & Riggio 2012). As a charismatic leader, you must always remember who you are in order not lose sight of what matters most even when times get tough on your path towards achieving change.

Humility plays a pivotal role in balancing charisma preventing it from veering into narcissism or arrogance. Humble leaders acknowledge their own limitations while recognizing contributions made by others thereby creating a culture that promotes collaboration respect empathy among team members (bass & Riggio 2012). By being humble, one makes every person feel valued since they are given equal chances to participate in decision making processes leading to increased engagement productivity.

To strike the right balance between charisma, humility, and authenticity it is necessary to avoid potential pitfalls or negative consequences associated with over-reliance on charisma. One common pitfall is becoming overly dependent on personal charm without cultivating substance or competency. Charismatic leaders must understand that charisma alone cannot guarantee long-term success; instead it needs to be accompanied by hard work and dedication towards improving oneself continuously so as to achieve sustainable results throughout one's career lifespan irrespective to any challenges met along the way (bass & Riggio 2012).

Manipulation or exploitation may also be a potential problem. Charismatic leaders have the power to profoundly influence others; however, it is crucial that this authority is exercised ethically and responsibly. With reference to how they affect others, leaders must not abuse the trust of those following them, nor should they use followers for their own gain. By focusing on the common good and serving the best interests of their teams, such leaders can avoid these pitfalls.

"great leaders inspire, exceptional leaders listen".

Chapter 10

SERVANT LEADERSHIP: LEADING WITH EMPATHY AND COMPASSION:

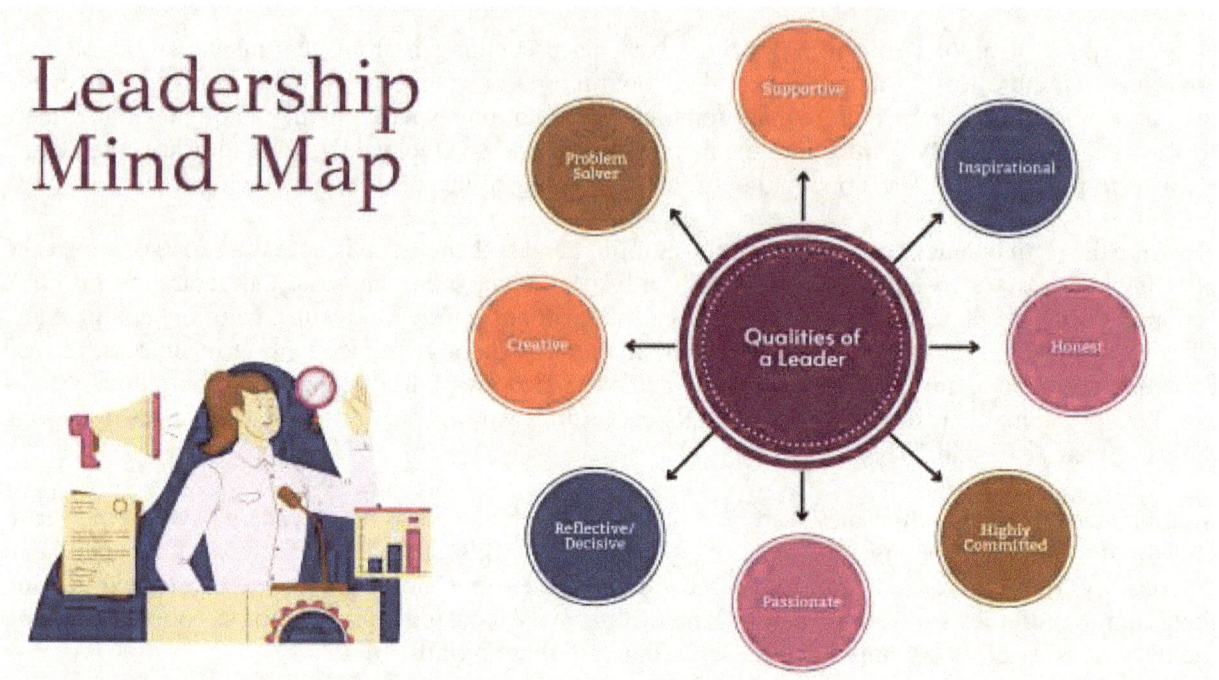

Servant leadership is a leadership style that stresses on serving others and putting others before themselves. It is based on the notion that leaders should focus on the welfare and growth of their followers rather than their selfish interests or desire for power. What defines servant leaders is their empathy and compassion, enabling them to connect with team members on a deeper level.

This chapter will delve into the concept of servant leadership in depth by examining its principles as well as its connection to compassion and empathy. The significance of truly understanding what their followers go through is something that servant leaders appreciate. By having deep empathy for others, they can relate better with their teammates in more meaningful ways thus creating a supportive inclusive work environment.

Another key characteristic of servant leadership is compassion which goes beyond mere sympathy to actively caring about the welfare of others. Compassionate leaders not only understand what their subordinates are going through but also make efforts to reduce their pain while supporting them in achieving self-growth. They show genuine concern for the happiness and success of those whom they lead thereby fostering trust-based collaborations among employees.

Throughout this chapter we will discuss practical strategies for developing empathy and compassion as qualities of leadership. We shall look at some case studies or examples where people have successfully demonstrated servant leadership through empathy or compassion so as to highlight how it works in practice. By understanding how leading with empathy and compassion can help shape organizational culture, we can see that there are positive outcomes which may arise from implementing this type of approach.

Adopting the principles of servant leadership along with incorporating empathy and compassion into one's own style can greatly benefit aspiring transformational leaders as well. By prioritizing the needs of others, leaders can foster respect, trust, collaboration cultures among staff which inspire them towards achieving collective goals.

The role of empathy in servant leadership:

Empathy, which is a core quality of servant leadership plays a vital role in understanding and connecting with followers. Leaders can gain deeper insights into the perspectives, needs, and emotions of others by empathizing with them. This understanding helps them respond accordingly and offer support to facilitate growth or development as required.

In the context of servant leadership, empathy is not limited to mere sympathy or feeling sorry for someone else's misfortune; instead it extends beyond that through actively putting oneself into another person's shoes so as to feel what he/she feels from inside. As such, leaders who possess this ability are able to build trust and rapport with their team members creating an atmosphere whereby everyone feels safe enough to speak up without fear of being misunderstood or ignored because they know they would be appreciated by someone else on staff.

When leaders show empathy towards others, they are acknowledging that people have different difficulties and experiences in life. They tend to listen carefully while seeking understanding thus validating emotions expressed by followers. Therefore, these actions form a basis for establishing trust relationships within organizations where transparency and open communication prevail.

Moreover, empathetic leaders pay attention not only to what their subordinates say but also how they say it through body language, tone of voice etc.. For instance; during interactions there may be some non-verbal cues like facial expressions showing happiness, sadness etc. Thus being aware of such signs helps one to better interpret and meet the various emotional requirements of his/her employees.

Additionally, empathy contributes to effective decision-making by building positive relationships. When leaders are empathetic, they consider how their decisions will affect others and look at things from different perspectives. This approach promotes fairness, equity, and inclusivity within the organization.

Creating a supportive and inclusive work environment is possible for servant leaders through incorporating empathy in their leadership style itself, at its core. They foster a culture where individuals feel comfortable expressing their opinions, seeking guidance, and working collaboratively towards shared goals. The emphasis on empathy helps break down barriers, reduce conflicts, and encourage cooperation among team members.

In order to be a servant leader who cultivates empathy it is important that we learn to practice active listening and show genuine interest in others. This entails having meaningful conversations with people asking open-ended questions as well as encouraging them to share what they are thinking or feeling about something that concerns them. By doing this the leader can gain more insights into his/her employees' experiences thereby creating an environment where everyone feels valued.

Empathy is not a fixed trait but can be cultivated through deliberate practice. Feedback is one method by which servant leaders improve their capacity to empathize while reflecting on personal biases allow them to identify areas where understanding might be lacking due to cultural differences among other things (Northouse 2016). Engaging employees in exercises like role-playing scenarios or putting them through empathy-focused training programs also enhances their ability to see things from someone else's perspective.

To sum up, empathy plays a vital role in servant leadership by fostering understanding, connection, and trust between leaders and followers (spears 1995). Leaders who empathize with others create an environment where collaboration flourishes because everyone feels supported within such a setting leading to personal growth initiatives being undertaken collectively for the betterment of all (Greenleaf

1977). Therefore, this caring way of leadership contributes towards both individual wellbeing as well organizational and transformational success.

Developing compassion as a servant leader:

Another key quality of a servant leader beside empathy is cultivating compassion. Unlike empathy which is about understanding someone's feelings or point of view, compassion means genuinely caring for their welfare and success. Thus a compassionate servant leader prioritizes his/her employees' needs while actively searching for means through which they can be aided.

There are several practical strategies that servant leaders can implement to develop and strengthen compassion as a leadership quality:

1. Cultivate self-compassion: before extending compassion towards others, it is important for servant leaders first practice self-care. This entails treating oneself kindly rather than harshly regardless of any mistakes committed; accepting one's limitations instead of striving for perfectionism. By doing so they will create a foundation upon which extending sympathy becomes possible.

2. Practice active listening: for compassionate leadership, active listening plays a crucial role. Servant leaders should therefore listen attentively when people speak without rushing into quick conclusions or judgments, but rather seek understanding from their viewpoints and emotions fully (Northouse 2016). This way they show real concern about connecting with team members at deeper levels beyond mere surface conversations.

3. Foster a culture of psychological safety: building psychological safety within teams is essential if compassion has to thrive among them. Trust and support are key elements in an atmosphere where individuals feel secure enough to share what they think, feel like or go through regarding certain issues without being afraid that others will criticize them badly afterwards (Luthans & Avolio 2003). In such cases leaders practice authentic listening validating emotions offering guidance whenever necessary and thus allowing compassion to flourish further as well.

4. Compassionate leadership starts at the top, leading by example. As a servant leader, you have to act compassionately in everything that you do. This includes being kind, showing respect and empathy for others in your team, recognizing their achievements and efforts, and giving feedback in a compassionate way. By doing so, other people within that organization will also want to follow suit thus creating a ripple effect of compassion.

5. Value collaboration and teamwork: compassionate leaders understand the importance of working together as a team towards achieving common goals. They actively promote an environment that encourages cooperation, open communication and mutual support among team members. In this light, servant leaders create opportunities for individuals to come together, share ideas and collectively problem-solve which further nurtures compassion within the team.

6. Growth and development opportunities: compassionate leaders are invested in their team members' growth and success. These may include personal & professional development opportunities like mentoring programs or coaching sessions among others aimed at improving their skills set so they can become the better professionals of tomorrow rather than yesterday. Therefore it shows that through investing in the team's growth these kinds of leaders show their care toward them as well as a commitment toward their long-term success.

7. Be grateful: being thankful is another way whereby servant leaders can show love & compassion too. Thanking people who work with us builds them up making them feel part of that family, or group. Bad relationships contrastingly are characterized by little recognition whereby individuals fail to connect positively with the leader's vision hence leading to isolation and poor commitment to transformation or change.

By implementing these strategies, servant leaders can develop and strengthen their capacity for compassion, leading to a more empathetic and supportive work environment. Furthermore, by modeling compassionate behaviors and creating opportunities for growth, servant leaders inspire their teams to embody compassion themselves creating a positive cycle of empathy and care that permeates throughout the organization.

Leading with empathy and compassion is a powerful approach to leadership that emphasizes the importance of understanding and serving others.

In addition to promoting collaboration, a culture of empathy and compassion also cultivates trust among team members. When leaders genuinely care about the personal and professional growth of their employees it builds trust & loyalty within the organization whereby people feel valued respected supported since they know that their leader is really concerned with their success. This trust creates a positive work environment where individuals are more willing to take risks, share their ideas, and contribute to the collective goals of the organization.

Employee satisfaction is another vital aspect that servant leadership and empathy and compassion culture influence, reducing absenteeism, work to rule and staff turnover, all key drains on productivity and business growth.

In general, servant leadership together with an empathetic and compassionate culture has a transformative effect on the organization. Through prioritizing others' needs, leaders encourage collaboration, trust and make employees satisfied while at work. A culture of this nature leads to higher levels of engagement, productivity as well as innovation within the organization.

Servant leadership: leading with empathy and compassion: case studies and examples:

In this section we are going to take a look at some real life examples where leaders have effectively demonstrated servant leadership through empathy together with compassion. These leaders act as strong role models who show how leading with empathy and compassion can result in positive outcomes that have long lasting effects.

A case in point is nelson Mandela who was south Africa's former president having also been a prominent human rights' defender. Mandela displayed an exceptional level of empathy coupled with compassion throughout his leadership journey especially when he struggled to end apartheid rule in order to unite people from different races living in one country divided by hatred (Willard & Kernis 2016). Despite suffering for many years due to imprisonment plus other hardships Mandela chose forgiveness over revenge thereby epitomizing what these values mean (Hofmeyr et al., 2015). He managed to earn respect from people all over the world by showing that he could feel the pain of even those who oppressed him including their families.

Another example of a great leader who embodies servant leadership through empathy and compassion is Mary Barra, CEO of general motors. Barra has always shown genuine concern for her subordinates' welfare thus creating a culture that upholds these virtues within the company (Wollard & Kernis 2016). When faced with the ignition switch scandal back in 2014; she acted swiftly to handle this crisis while prioritizing safety of both customers and employees. This way she managed not only to restore public trust but also to motivate workers towards working together so as to get back on track (Hofmeyr et al., 2015).

Furthermore, dr. Paul farmer co-founder of partners in health (PIH) is another example of servant leader who exemplifies this trait through his unwavering commitment towards providing healthcare services for less privileged communities across different parts of the globe. Farmer's approach is deeply rooted in empathy and compassion as he advocates for social justice and equity in healthcare. By tirelessly working hard on behalf of patients from poorer backgrounds irrespective of their social economic status farmer has changed many lives by ensuring they receive quality medical attention when needed (Wollard & Kernis 2016).

These case studies indicate how servant leaders who prioritize empathy along with compassion can make significant positive changes within their organizations as well as within their communities at large. (Hofmeyer et al., 2015).

These examples provide valuable lessons for us as aspiring transformational leaders. If we make empathy and compassion the basis of our leadership style, we will be able to establish deep connections with our team members. Thus, they will feel motivated to achieve their goals. By showing genuine concern for others and providing assistance when needed, we can facilitate individual growth and encourage creativity, which are essential factors for maintaining business prosperity.

As you can see the servant leadership style has a great deal of overlap with effective transformational leadership and all effective transformational leader display elements of this style, however other leadership styles also overlap with the role of transformational leadership and can also help promote a catalyst for change.

Chapter 11

TRANSACTIONAL LEADERSHIP: BALANCING REWARDS AND EXPECTATIONS

In chapter 11 we will explore transactional leadership in detail by examining its key characteristics as well as the role played by rewards and expectations in this style of leadership.

This chapter focuses on transactional leadership which is characterized by contingent reward – the provision of benefits from leaders to employees based on meeting predetermined performance objectives (Northouse, 2018). Meanwhile there are also other issues that arise when discussing this topic such as how managers should manage their subordinates during emergencies or what they should do when there is a conflict between two employees who are equally competent in terms of skills but have different attitudes towards work.

The role played by transactional leaders is that they establish clear expectations and performance standards for their followers. In contrast, transformational leaders inspire and empower individuals to achieve higher levels of performance through personal growth (Northouse, 2018). They do this by setting specific goals and providing structure within which people know exactly what is expected from them.

Transactional leadership can only be understood in terms of its exchange relationship between the leader and subordinates. A special type called contingent reward involves giving rewards to followers once certain performance standards are met while management-by-exception requires close monitoring of employee activities so as to avoid deviations from established norms (bass & Riggio, 2006). Moreover, a reward system is devised which corresponds with desired outcomes and acts as an incentive for people to put forth their best efforts in order to attain them.

Apart from contingent reward, transactional leaders also use the management-by-exception approach. Under this method, the leader closely observes how his followers perform without intervening unless something goes wrong thereby ensuring that everything runs smoothly (Avolio & bass, 2004). Transactional leadership entails being proactive in identifying problems then solving them so as to keep performance on track.

Although transactional leadership may be effective under certain circumstances; however it should strike a balance between rewards and expectations. Overemphasis on rewarding can create an entitlement culture where individuals expect too much from their superiors without contributing anything towards the achievement of organizational objectives (bass & Riggio, 2006). Conversely, excessive expectations without adequate recognition or rewards may decrease motivation and satisfaction among followers.

To find a balance between rewards and expectations effectively; transactional leaders must first create clear expectations' systems within their organizations. This can only be achieved through effective communication of goals, visions and performance standards by leaders thus enabling their followers to know exactly what is required from them (avolio & bass, 2004). Consequently, people can align their efforts with desired outcomes thereby improving goal attainment.

Furthermore, rewards must be used appropriately by transactional leader's so as to motivate employees. These may include financial incentives like bonuses or commissions as well as recognition items such as plaques or certificates and chances for career advancement among others (bass & riggio, 2006).

Leaders should tailor these enticements to suit individual wants and interests since different individuals get motivated by different things.

Transactional leadership offers a structured form of management that can work well in some situations. However, balance has to be struck between rewards and expectations by these leaders who seek to motivate their followers towards achieving organizational objectives while ensuring fairness during the process (Northouse, 2018). Therefore, subsequent sections within this chapter will delve deeper into creating clear expectations' systems and leveraging rewards effectively which are two practical strategies aimed at helping enhance leadership effectiveness among those using transactional style.

The framework of transactional leadership is based on the principles of rewarding and giving consequences to followers depending on their performance. Contingent reward and management-by-exception are two major components of this framework that significantly influence the behaviors of followers.

According to bass (1990), transactional leadership is a form of management that bases its actions on external rewards and punishments. Unlike transformational leadership that inspires and empowers individuals, transactional leaders work within an exchange system (bass & Riggio, 2006). However, a transformational leader can use rewards as well and indeed often there is a transition period between moving from a transactional business model to a transformational one.

Remember that transactional leaders are known for their ability to establish clear expectations and performance standards for their subordinates. Such leaders believe that people are primarily motivated by external incentives such as rewards or punishments but not intrinsic factors (bass & Riggio, 2006). Through setting objectives with specificity together with providing structure, transactional leaders create a situation whereby followers know exactly what they should do, this can be useful when dealing with a poorly educated or motivated workforce, and may be a necessary step until motivation improves through cultural change.

Central theme of transactional leadership revolves around leader-follower exchange relationship. A key feature in this kind of relationship is contingent reward where rewards are provided to subordinates upon meeting predetermined performance criteria (bass & Riggio, 2006).

Furthermore, transactional leaders develop a reward system which corresponds to desired outcomes and encourages employees' topmost performance levels, again this is useful where the transformational leader has suspicions many do not buy into their vision, indeed changing an organizations culture can take significant time and effort, as a stop-gap measure transformational leaders can employ tactics from the transactional leaders wheelhouse in order to buy time to promote the change that is needed.

Apart from contingent reward, transactional leaders also employ a management-by-exception approach. Under this approach, follower's performance is closely monitored while interventions are only made in case there are deviations from established standards (Avolio & bass, 2004). Transactional leadership involves being proactive in identifying problems then solving them so as to keep performance on track, in this aspect their is some similarity, but contrastingly with transformational leadership most interactions are negative in nature i.e. 'correcting' errors, rather than change seeking in and of themselves.

Transactional leadership can be effective in some contexts; however, it is important to find a balance between rewards and expectations. Overemphasis on rewarding may lead to entitlement culture or short-term thinking where individuals concentrate on earning rewards rather than long-term goals (bass & Riggio, 2006). Conversely, excessive expectations without adequate recognition or rewards may decrease motivation and satisfaction among followers.

For transactional leaders to balance between rewards and expectations effectively, they must first establish a system of clear expectations. Leaders achieve this clarity by communicating the vision, goals and performance standards of their organizations thus making it easier for their followers to understand what is required of them (Avolio & bass, 2004). Consequently, people can align their efforts with desired outcomes thereby improving goal attainment likelihood.

Moreover, rewards must be used by transactional leader's appropriately. These may include financial incentives like bonuses or commissions as well as recognition items such as plaques or certificates and chances for career advancement among others (bass & Riggio, 2006). Leaders should tailor these enticements to suit individual wants and interests since different individuals get motivated by different things.

Transactional leadership provides a structured form of management that works well in certain situations. By balancing between rewards and expectations, transactional leaders motivate their followers to achieve organizational objectives while ensuring fairness during the process (bass & Riggio, 2006).

On the other hand, management-by-exception entails closely monitoring follower performance and intervening only when there are deviations from set standards. Transactional leaders who use this style also create boundaries for their followers by putting up certain rules and regulations that guide them in their conduct. They will intervene whenever a follower fails to meet the requirements or something happens which calls for corrective measures, it is common for these boundaries to involve things such as best practice handbooks and instructions to not deviate from a users role or prescribed tasks, whilst useful sometimes, these prescriptions provide a barrier to change catalysts looking to drive transformation through discouraging the risk-taker mindset, companies that employee transactional managers often do quite well, but rarely are exceptional or groundbreaking.

A combination of contingent rewards and management-by-exception establishes a system where followers are motivated through both positive reinforcement and negative consequences. Expectations were effectively communicated by these leaders; rewards distribution was clarified while performance problems were addressed instantly. This kind of framework is designed to create an atmosphere in which people strive towards perfection using both carrots (rewards) & sticks (punishments).

However, it is important to note that transactional leadership mainly concentrates on immediate results achieved through either rewards or punishments. It cannot foster creativity, innovation or long term exponential growth because its focus is mainly on doing things as per-say rather than encouraging exploration & risk taking. Nonetheless, when well balanced with other forms of leadership styles it can contribute positively towards creating a productive organizational culture characterized by good if not outstanding performance.

Transactional leadership: balancing rewards and expectations:

This section focuses on balancing rewards with expectations within the context of transactional leadership as a stop gap to a transformational management style. While transactional leadership relies on a system of rewards and consequences to motivate followers, finding the right equilibrium between these two elements is essential for effective leadership.

As transactional leaders, it is imperative that we strike a balance between providing incentives and setting clear expectations. When rewards are overemphasized without corresponding expectations, it can create a culture of entitlement and undermine accountability. On the other hand, if expectations are excessively emphasized without adequate recognition or rewards, it can lead to demotivation, dissatisfaction, and even burnout among followers.

Finding this delicate equilibrium requires a nuanced understanding of individual needs and motivations. It entails recognizing that different individuals may respond differently to various types of rewards and expectations. Effective transactional leaders take the time to understand their followers, identifying what drives them and tailoring rewards and expectations accordingly.

Rewards can come in different forms like financial incentives, recognition, career growth opportunities etc. It is important to ensure fairness and transparency when rewarding because an unfair or inconsistent reward system can create bitterness and mistrust among followers thereby eroding the effectiveness of transactional leadership, golf course politics and weekend drinking sessions with the boss type scenarios are clear examples where apparent unfairness in a company's reward structure can undermine motivation and productivity alike.

Equally important is establishing clear expectations and performance standards. When followers know what is expected of them, they can align their efforts better. Transactional leaders should effectively communicate these expectations by clarifying the desired outcomes and specifying the behaviors or actions required to achieve them.

However, one must be careful not to set unrealistic or unachievable expectations. Overwhelming subordinates with excessive demands results in stress, decreased morale and ultimately poor performance. A balanced approach to expectations setting takes into consideration individual capabilities and resources while still challenging followers to reach their full potential.

Throughout this chapter we will examine some of the possible problems that may arise from overemphasizing rewards or expectations. We will look at ways of striking a delicate balance between the two so that transactional leaders can effectively motivate their followers while maintaining fairness, transparency and accountability.

Creating a system of clear expectations:

One major responsibility you have as a transactional leader is establishing clear expectations for your followers regarding their behavior and performance levels. This gives them a sense of direction which eventually leads towards goal attainment as well as motivational factors.

To create a system of clear expectations consider using these strategies:

1. Clearly define goals: start by stating specific goals that are in line with your organization's mission statement or vision document; then communicate these objectives down towards all employees making sure they fully understand what needs accomplishing; use precise language together with examples or benchmarks if necessary so that everyone gets it right.
2. Set measurable targets: divide larger objectives into smaller achievable targets; this enables followers to monitor their progress and feel a sense of achievement each time they hit any milestone; make sure your targets are measurable enough for individuals to effectively track their performance within the given timeframe.
3. Communicate performance standards: indicate clearly what performance standards will be relied upon when assessing individual or team output; give specific guidelines on successful performance criteria as well as metrics used in determining such an outcome; this way, nobody can claim ignorance about his/her role in the organization.
4. Solicit input and feedback: regularly engage with subordinates so that you discuss how they perceive these expectations together with performance measures; let them ask questions if confused about anything while seeking clarification when necessary; by doing so, you would address any misunderstanding before it affects productivity levels since you value their opinions too much not to listen actively.
5. Provide resources and support: ensure that your followers have all necessary resources required for meeting established criteria including tools, training materials etc.; lack of these could impede progress causing frustrations among employees; hence, it falls upon those following a transactional leadership style even temporarily to break down barriers hindering performance growth thus facilitating success through provision of adequate backing.
6. Progress monitoring: develop mechanisms for reviewing progress towards set goals and standards. Continually evaluate the performance of individuals and teams, giving feedback on areas where improvement is needed as well as highlighting strengths. Deal with successes adequately and quickly attend to fears to maintain progress and motivation.

Creating a system with clear expectations has more benefits than just achieving objectives. When you are clear, it creates transparency which brings about trust with your followers. If you have outlined what is expected of them, then they are motivated in order to meet those expectations leading to increased accountability.

These strategies lay the foundation for effective transactional leadership that balances rewards and expectations. Remember that transactional leaders followers are motivated by clear communication and knowing what is expected from them in order to achieve organizational goals.

Rewards balancing transactional leadership:

In this part of the chapter on transactional leadership, we will discuss how rewards can be effectively used by transactional leaders. Rewards serve as motivators while also reinforcing desired behaviors among followers and performance standards as well.

There are different types of rewards available for transactional leaders including financial incentives such as bonuses based on commission or pay determined by results achieved; recognition through words spoken publicly about someone's achievement; or even simple actions like writing thank you notes personally given out during meetings). In fact each type has its unique value proposition making it possible to align rewards with your organization's objectives.

Transactional leadership often uses financial incentives when rewarding its members for achievements made under their watch. These include commissions earned from sales made by employees or bonuses paid out after meeting certain targets within stipulated periods. Such incentives bring immediate gains hence act as great motivators particularly if linked directly towards accomplishing specific aims set beforehand.

Another reward that works well for transactional leaders is recognition. In fact appreciating somebody's input either in the form of an award ceremony held once yearly where all winners across different categories receive certificates together with cheques worth significant money or else through simple gestures like writing a thankyou letter addressed directly towards the recipient. However, fairness must prevail at all times especially when dealing with rewards because some individuals could feel left out despite having done a good job throughout the year simply because they were not favored more than others, remember perceptions are important.

Apart from that, career progression also forms part of a valuable rewards culture for followers. Offering advancement opportunities such as promotions; additional responsibilities; access development programs indicate to subordinates that management recognizes their efforts made so far would like to see them grow even further professionally. Consequently, it becomes crucial task leaders identify high potential employees within a group while at same time providing guidance on how best they can achieve these aspirations hence investing into long-term wellbeing such individuals. This is perhaps the reward most akin to transformational leadership styles.

While utilizing rewards in transactional leadership is crucial for motivating followers, it is equally important for leaders to maintain fairness and transparency. Rewards should be allocated based on objective criteria and performance standards that are well-communicated to all members of the team. This helps prevent any perception of favoritism or inequality among followers. Additionally, leaders should regularly reassess and adjust their reward systems to ensure they remain relevant and aligned with the evolving needs and goals of the organization.

By using effective rewards, transactional leaders can create a positive working environment where employees feel appreciated because their contributions are recognized thereby leading to increased motivation. However, it is essential that managers strike the right balance between reward packages. Leaders need to understand the fact that though incentives may drive short term results; developing intrinsic motivation coupled with a true sense of purpose remains the key driver to sustainable growth in the long run and this is made possible by evolving the leadership style and business culture.

How to remain authentic when starting with a transactional style and then evolving:

The world somewhere along the way has lost sight of what true leadership means. Our organizations, political structures, schools, and communities have all suffered due to a lack of effective leadership. This void has been felt from the top-down in both our personal and professional lives. However, these answers are not as hard to find as they may seem.

In a world that is constantly changing for better or worse, there remains one thing that should never change – our core values. However, in recent times we have found it difficult to identify and uphold these values. As we pull away from our values everything starts feeling transactional, lacking any meaning or purpose. We push people away when we focus only on ourselves instead of thinking about everyone else's well-being. It is time for us to shift gears and take up transformational leadership.

Understanding the value of core values:

Core values represent those guiding principles that help define who we are and how we act. They serve as a context for interaction between us and the surrounding world. Honesty, confidence, perseverance, kindness and humility are universally accepted positive traits that every effective leader must have.

These include Steve jobs who attributed his success on living by them; it was believed by jobs that intelligence direction coupled with hard work supplemented with enthusiasm and passion were the key ingredients towards achieving greatness amongst other things similarity life lived according to core values equips one with ability lead fulfilling life meaningful contribution towards others' lives.

Mahatma Gandhi once said "values become our destiny." As such through embracing these principles which make us what we are today thus determine where we will finally land on earth.

Cultivating a transformational culture:

Culture plays an important role in shaping organizations and communities as well. A transformational leader knows how imperative it is to create culture which fosters growth through innovation while encouraging collaboration at the same time. By investing in individuals' welfare leaders can foster creativity within an environment that allows for self-direction and personal development.

For instance, zappos is a model company that offers comprehensive benefits to its employees, practices self-management and encourages creativity (Olguin, 2013). Not only does this approach enhance employee satisfaction but also drives innovation leading ultimately into success.

In a transformational culture people come first because their well-being and growth are key determinants of overall organizational success.

Investing in people: putting others first:

Leaders must remember that they cannot succeed alone but with others too; hence as leaders we need support from other team members who contribute towards the achievement of our goals.

There is no better way to be a good leader other than by valuing relationships. This means that every new opportunity and creative endeavor are often borne out by time-consuming strong relationships. Napoleon hill's book "think and grow rich" tells a story of Edwin Barnes who showed an unbreakable spirit when he sought employment from Thomas Edison. Eventually, dedication paid off in a big way as the young man became a millionaire.

To become a transformational leader, one has to invest time and effort into building mutually beneficial relationships. These connections provide avenues for growth, collaboration, and opportunity. So how do we stay true to our transformative nature when we enter a leadership role within an organization with a culture of transactional leadership?

Step 0: relax and breathe:

Get to know the company and the people, talk to them about change and engage with their feedback positively, make sure your colleagues know they are valued, look at ways to build trust and display empathy, then when the time is right seek out change.

Step 1: lead with your values:

In order to embark on the journey towards transformational leadership it is important that one leads with their values. We are defined by what we do, and our values shape the choices we make as well as guide our relationships with others. Select core values that resonate with you and build your life upon them. Living with honesty, integrity, kindness, and respect will not only win you admiration but also enhance your own life too.

Step 2: foster a transformational culture:

Creating a transformational culture requires investing in people's well-being first before anything else. Encourage creativity, self-direction and personal growth within your organization or community. By offering comprehensive benefits, promoting self-management, and fostering an environment of innovation, you can cultivate a culture that inspires others.

Step 3: invest in people:

For instance, allocating your most valuable resource-time towards improving oneself by adding value onto other people's lives through mentorship programs; or volunteering in internal business career workshops.

Step 4: nurture meaningful relationships:

Building strong relationships is essential for transformational leadership. Dedicate time and effort towards developing connections that are mutually beneficial. These relationships will open doors to new opportunities, collaborations, and personal growth. Remember, being a follower is not a bad thing; it is through learning from others and forming meaningful relationships that we become effective leaders.

The movement from transactional leadership style to transformational leadership requires conscious efforts put in place such as leading with values, fostering transformation culture, investing people as well as nurturing meaningful relationships. By embracing these principles one can inspire others while at the same time empowering themselves hence creating lasting impact within their societies.

Embrace the journey of transformational leadership remembering that you should remain faithful unto thyself; invest in humanity's development by making friends who matter most for life long partnerships where trust reigns supreme always. By doing so you will not only become a successful leader and catalyst for change.

Chapter 12

AUTHENTIC LEADERSHIP: EMBRACING YOUR TRUE SELF TO INSPIRE OTHERS

Recently, authentic leadership has become a buzzword in the field of charismatic leadership. In essence, it entails a style of leadership that focuses on being true to oneself and displaying genuine conducts. Authentic leaders are not shy to embrace their real selves and bring their whole person to their roles. They grasp the necessity of harmonizing values, beliefs, and actions within themselves thereby help them inspire others.

Authentic leadership has emerged as a powerful approach for driving meaningful change and building trust with followers in today's world where authenticity and transparency are highly valued. This goes beyond conventional understanding of leadership that may be more concerned with image over actual connection with others.

What distinguishes authentic leaders is their capacity to lead from self-awareness. They have a profound insight into their strengths, weaknesses, values, and motivations. Through this self-awareness, they can be truthful both to themselves and others consequently creating an environment characterized by trust and psychological safety.

However, embracing one's true self in leadership requires vulnerability; which means being willing to show up as the person you really are even though you might face judgment or criticism from others. Furthermore, authentic leaders understand that authenticity attracts authenticity hence if they desire genuine open followers then they must first practice vulnerability.

Moreover, embracing oneself as a leader means recognizing individual differences as well as respecting them. For instance authentic leaders promote diversity such as inclusivity so that everyone feels seen heard valued just for who they truly are while at work place.

Authentic leadership is not about trying to conform to a particular mold or fit into preconceived notions of what a leader should be. Instead it encourages leaders to embrace their unique qualities perspectives experiences etc as sources strength; thereby inspiring others do same thus create culture celebrating individuality fostering creativity innovation within organization.

What is the difference between authentic leadership and transformational leadership?

Leadership is very important for the success of any organization. Despite the many theories and approaches to leadership, two styles that have gained attention in recent years are authentic leadership and transformational leadership. While both styles aim to inspire and motivate followers, they differ in principles and focus as will be explored through examining their key characteristics, effects on employee behavior, and mediating role of job satisfaction.

Authentic leadership:

Authentic leadership theory is a relatively new leadership theory which stresses the significance of personal traits and values in a leader. It is based on the idea that those leaders who stay true to themselves and exhibit such qualities as transparency, ethics, self-awareness, and balanced processing can certainly encourage their subordinates. In line with Avolio and Gardner (2005), authentic leadership draws from positive psychological capacities and highly developed organizational context resulting in greater self-awareness as well as positive behaviors among leaders plus their associates.

Self-awareness:

One fundamental component of authentic leadership is self-awareness. It entails having an understanding of one's strengths, weaknesses, values by a leader who keeps working on his or herself constantly. With regard to actions performed by self-aware leaders they are conscious how these affect others thereby leading better relationships that are more real.

Transparency:

Another key aspect regarding authentic leadership is transparency. Leaders who are transparent openly share information, thoughts, emotions with their followers. Trust engagement and open dialogue fostered by these individuals through communicating authentically ensures authenticity within an organization. This is balanced by transformational leaders that empathize with employees and use open communication, but whom might not always be as candid with employees.

Ethics and morals:

When looking at authentic leadership ethics/morals play a significant role here. Authentic leaders stick to internal moral standards guiding them while they make decisions even if there exist external pressures on them. They prioritize ethical behavior and thus demonstrate integrity thereby setting examples for followers who would do likewise. Transformational leaders may often find themselves at odds with their companies pre-existing culture deciding to be catalysts for change from the inside out. Authentic leaders do not compromise even temporarily on their leadership style and o may struggle to change a deeply rooted transactional culture for example.

Balanced processing:

Balanced processing stands for being objective during decision making processes. Authentic leaders seek input from diverse perspectives and other workers before making decisions. They value different viewpoints and are open to challenging their own beliefs and convictions thereby creating an inclusive work environment that fosters collaboration.

Transformational leadership verses authentic leadership:

Transformational leadership focuses on inspiring and transforming followers in order to achieve exceptional results. It comprises four main components: idealized influence, intellectual stimulation, inspirational motivation and individualized consideration.

Idealized influence:

Idealized influence refers to how a leader can become a role model hence gaining admiration and respect from his/her followers. Transformational leaders inspire others through high ethical standards, values and consistent behavior.

Intellectual stimulation:

This involves challenging the status quo by encouraging creativity and innovation among followers. This is notably not part of the authentic leadership role and is unique to transformational leaders and change catalysts. Transformational leaders stimulate critical thinking and problem solving as well as continued learning opportunities, which creates culture continuous improvement and growth within an organization.

Inspirational motivation:

Inspirational motivation is a key component in transformational leadership where leaders inspire and motivate their followers through creating a vision, setting high expectations, and giving purpose and meaning to the work done by their teams. Inspirational motivation means that transformational leaders create compelling visions establish lofty goals and objectives.

Individualized consideration:

This involves treating each follower differently because they are unique individuals who have different needs, strengths and development opportunities. Transformational leaders act as mentors, coaches and provide support, guidance and personalized attention to help their followers grow and reach their full potential.

Effects on employee behavior:

Both authentic leadership and transformational leadership have been shown to positively affect employee behavior as well as organizational outcomes.

Organizational citizenship behavior (OCB):

Organizational citizenship behavior (OCB) refers to discretionary behaviors that go beyond the formal job requirements and contribute to the overall effectiveness and well-being of the organization. Two dimensions of OCB that are especially applicable to authentic and transformational leadership styles include altruism, as well as general compliance.

Altruism:

This involves acts of helping and supporting others within the workplace without expecting anything in return. It has been discovered through studies that authentic leadership and transformational leadership influences positively on employee altruism since such leaders consider their followers' welfare as well as create a culture characterized by empathy and support.

General compliance:

This represents a kind of behavior that follows formal job requirements or organizational rules. However, while there is no direct link between authentic leadership and general compliance, some researchers have found out that transformational leadership leads to more general compliant behavior among employees. This is because transformational leaders provide high expectations for their followers with clear guidance leading them towards higher levels of obedience.

The role of job satisfaction:

Job satisfaction plays an important role in mediating the relationship between different types of leadership styles and employee behaviors. Previous research has shown a positive correlation between job satisfaction and both authentic leadership and transformational leadership styles.

Authentic leadership and job satisfaction:

Job satisfaction is significantly influenced by authentic leadership. This means that when leaders act genuinely, transparently, and ethically employees develop trust which results in increased engagement and work satisfaction. Authenticity leads to higher levels of commitment and motivation. Job satisfaction also contributes towards increased overall welfare and feelings of commitment outside of work reducing absenteeism.

Transformational leadership and job satisfaction:

There is also a strong positive relationship between transformational leadership and job satisfaction. This is because transformational leaders create positive work climates by inspiring followers through motivation as well purpose. Employee-job fit is critical in enhancing employees' perception about their transformational leaders. Such employees are more likely to have high levels of job satisfaction if they feel valued, supported, and challenged by their leaders who give them opportunities to develop, advance, give meaningful feedback and take risk.

Job satisfaction as a mediator:

Job satisfaction acts as a mediator between various leadership styles and employee behaviors such as OCB. In this case, satisfied workers are more likely to engage themselves with any activities that can contribute towards organizational success such as altruism and general compliance because they are already happy with what they do. Job satisfaction bridges the gap between leadership styles, outcomes and employee behaviors thus increasing the positive effects of authentic and transformational leaderships upon employee's behavior within organizations at large.

Authentic leadership differs from transformational leadership though both are regarded as effective forms of leadership in modern organizations. Authentic leadership emphasizes personal traits, transparency, ethics and self-awareness while on the other hand transformational type focuses on inspiring or transforming followers through idealized influence, intellectual stimulation, inspirational motivation and individualized consideration. Both styles have been found to have positive effects on employee behavior including organizational citizenship behavior. By understanding the differences between authentic leadership and transformational leadership and their impact on employee behavior, organizations can cultivate effective leadership and create a positive work environment that fosters employee engagement, well-being, and organizational success.

Through leveraging personal values, leaders can develop an influential leadership style that encourages others to unleash their full potential. When leaders truly live according to what they believe in deeply at heart; it creates a ripple effect throughout their organization or team. Consequently, they empower team members who become inspired thereby creating an environment characterized by authenticity, integrity and purpose.

Chapter 13

TRANSFORMATIONAL LEADERSHIP IN NONPROFIT ORGANIZATIONS

Non-profit organizations face different obstacles that transformative leaders should navigate cautiously in order to bring about positive change. Among the obstacles that nonprofit leaders must overcome include limited resources, funding limitations, and stakeholders' management. These challenges will be explored in depth in this chapter with a special emphasis on how transformational leadership can provide solutions.

Among the primary challenges facing non-profit leadership is resource scarcity. Nonprofits usually work on very low budgets relying heavily on grants, donations as well as volunteers. This means that leadership roles might find it difficult to put up new programs or invest in the future.

Transformational leadership in nonprofit organizations: leveraging catalysts for social impact:

One key role played by catalysts is driving social impact and promoting positive change within nonprofit organizations. As transformational leaders, we need to know how to identify and nurture these catalysts so that they can inspire our teams as well as help us achieve our organization's mission.

Catalysts are dynamic elements that ignite change and inspire greatness while propelling teams towards success. When it comes to nonprofits, there could be many different things acting as catalysts; for instance some passionate individuals who understand underlying social issues deeply or possess skills which are unique enough such that without them; the goals set by the organization may not be achieved. They can also come out of innovative ideas developed into programs or initiatives which reshape the social change landscape.

Effective leveraging of these catalysts therefore begins with transformational leaders identifying them within their organization in the first instance. In other words, they are those persons, programs, tools, or resources which have shown unwavering commitment towards making a difference throughout the organization or which enable said difference to be achieved. Catalysts as people live their life at work because they know they have what it takes to inspire change, but most importantly; others must follow suit just like them if anything meaningful is going to happen at all, all people who are catalysts for change are leaders, but not all leaders are catalysts for change.

Once identified these people and resources should be nurtured by providing the necessary means through which they can be effectively utilized and thrive through activities such as funding allocations, professional growth opportunities, forming alliances with similar social partners either individuals or groups so that collectively they can bring about the desired change within and outside their organizations.

Moreover, such leaders need to regularly identify new catalysts through encouraging innovation and creativity among their teams. This involves developing a culture which appreciates different ways of thinking as well as encourages individuals to challenge existing norms with the view of coming up with better solutions instead. By doing this, it becomes possible for a leader to create an enabling environment where catalysts are nurtured hence unlocking the full potential of his/her organization towards driving social impact.

One thing that should be noted in this regard is that leveraging catalysts for social impact calls for intentional leadership strategies. For instance, transformational leaders should have a deep understanding regarding what their organizations stand for whereas at the same time promoting a clear vision related to any sought after changes. Through effective articulation of such visions; others can easily 'join the cause'.

Apart from identifying and nurturing catalysts, transformative leaders must also establish mechanisms through which collaboration and knowledge sharing can take place within their firms. This may include but not limited to setting up platforms meant for idea generation purposes; promoting cross functional teams or building community spirit among employees.

In general, transformational leaders in nonprofits who seek to drive social impact must be able to leverage catalysts, spot opportunities and nurture their resources. Transformational leaders can inspire their teams and achieve transformative change within their communities through their unwavering commitment to making a difference and by harnessing the power of influence, vision and empathy such leaders in nonprofits can create lasting social change and leave a legacy that resonates for years to come.

Overcoming barriers to transformational leadership in nonprofits:

Transformational leadership has the potential to make a significant impact in nonprofit organizations, driving positive change and inspiring teams to achieve their mission. However, like any leadership style, there can be barriers and resistance to implementing transformational leadership practices within nonprofit settings. In this section, we will explore some common barriers that nonprofit leaders may face and offer strategies and insights to overcome these obstacles.

One common barrier to transformational leadership in nonprofits is the fear of change. Many nonprofit organizations have established processes and procedures that have been in place for years. Implementing transformational leadership practices may require a shift in mindset and a willingness to embrace new approaches, something often difficult in an environment of scarce resources. This resistance to change can come from both leaders and employees who are comfortable with the status quo. To overcome this barrier, it is crucial for leaders to effectively communicate the benefits of transformational leadership and how it aligns with the organization's mission and goals. By emphasizing the positive impact that transformational leadership can have on the organization's ability to serve its constituents, leaders can help alleviate fears and gain support for implementing change.

Another barrier is limited resources among nonprofit organizations that inhibit them from practicing transformational leadership. Tight budgets are often experienced by non-profits thereby leading them to not being capable of implementing practices which could demand more time or money/investment such as organisation wide training programs. Leaders therefore need creativity when seeking means through which they would be able to utilize existing assets well, especially those connected with transformative initiatives so asto make them work despite the few resources at hand. This may call for reallocation or reprioritization of resources, seeking collaborative partnerships with other organizations as well as looking into alternative funding sources. By showing that they can be resourceful and think strategically, leaders will be able to overcome this issue and start implementing transformative leadership within their organizations.

Furthermore, there can be resistance from stakeholders at times which acts as another barrier towards transformational leadership in nonprofits. Some board members for instance could find it hard accepting changes while donors or volunteers might fear deviating from the norms they have always observed in the past. Such resistance might be because of either fear associated with uncertainty or due to a desire for maintaining control over where the organization is moving towards.

In order to address this barrier, leaders must ensure that they engage stakeholders so that there is open communication on how transformative leadership benefits them plus supports the mission of the charity or group. For instance, there can be holding town hall meetings, organizing workshops or volunteer-led trainings, among other ways through which these individuals would be given chances to speak their minds freely and thus help shape the decision making processes. By involving stakeholders in the processes of transformational leadership and addressing their concerns openly, leaders can build support for transformational leadership practices and overcome such resistance.

Another barrier to transformational leadership in nonprofits is a lack of leadership development and training opportunities. Nonprofit leaders are often passionate people who are deeply committed to their organization's mission but may not have had any formal leadership training. This can hinder their ability to effectively implement transformational leadership practices and utilize catalysts for change. To overcome this barrier, nonprofit leaders should seek professional development opportunities such as going for conferences, workshops or seminars on leadership development. They can also think about partnering with other organizations or getting mentorship from experienced leaders in the field who often provide free or subsidized trainings. By investing in their own personal growth and development, even in a more limited way, nonprofit leaders can develop the requisite skills and knowledge needed to effectively implement transformational leadership practices.

While there may be barriers and resistance to transformational leadership in non-profit organizations, it is necessary for leaders to navigate these challenges and establish a supportive climate for transformative practices. These barriers can be overcome by addressing fears of change, leveraging existing resources, engaging stakeholders, and investing in leadership development programs among other factors. In doing so, through perseverance and a commitment to creating lasting change; nonprofit leaders can inspire their teams, drive positive impacts as well as achieving the mission set forth by their organization changing society for the better.

Chapter 14

INTRODUCTION TO TRANSFORMATIONAL LEADERSHIP IN CORPORATE SETTINGS

David Ossip is a very successful entrepreneur, founder and CEO of Ceridian. This company provides human capital management software and services. David Ossip has been able to change the human resources (HR) function of organizations by creating products that enable employees to manage their own HR needs. In his own business David Ossip has reinvented business culture and driven employee engagement in a company that was previously under-performing.

Since joining Ceridian as CEO in 2013, David Ossip has transformed the company's organizational culture. Previously, it was a traditional top-down management style that focused on hierarchy and control. However, he introduced an innovative approach where decision-making is decentralized to teams rather than being done by individuals or a few executives at headquarters.

Additionally, this new culture encourages employees to take risks without fear of punishment from superiors because they have more freedom in making choices about what needs to be done within their respective departments without consulting higher authorities first. Moreover, it values open communication channels between management staff and team members on one side; and non-managerial workers on the other.

David Ossip, the CEO of Ceridian, had the challenge of reinventing the culture of a company with a disengaged workforce and declining business results. In recognizing that there was a need for better employee engagement to drive customer engagement and market share, ossip embarked on a transformative journey of change.

Ossip achieved this by focusing on aligning the organization's purpose with its values and creating a culture of transparency and communication. Ossip made employees have a sense of purpose by emphasizing customer focus, integrity, diligence and among other things he empowered them to make a difference with coaching on effective communication via programs like "top talent," with ideas being heard and employees feeling valued.

This has led to improved employee metrics for Ceridian which indicates a bright future ahead of them all because Ossip demonstrated transformational leadership. Therefore, through addressing foundational problems within the organization rather than treating symptoms only; Ceridian was set on success.

The complex reality of early transformational leadership:

Transformational leadership is an important catalyst for change in itself, but it is important to consider its complexities as well as potential pitfalls. Despite having their visionary qualities, leaders like Steve jobs were not always perfect either.

Jobs' aggressive behavior towards colleagues coupled with distorting reality raises questions about the darker side associated with charismatic leadership (bass & Riggio). Those employees who experienced wrath from job's aggression might work harder but at what cost? This is why empathy became included in recent developments in transformational leadership theory crossing some boundaries with the authentic leadership role.

Transformational leadership offers a pathway to redemption and change for corporations seeking to redefine their success. Leaders in the corporate world such as steve jobs or david ossip have demonstrated how much impact this kind of approach could have on organizations and industries at large scale and with a more empathetic nature transformative leaders of today can inspire even greater change and business success.

Although we have covered many aspects of this before we will now talk about how to effectively implement transformational leadership in a corporate setting, and what strategies leaders must consider. Think of this as revision as well as another foundational block in your learning journey.

To be effective in a corporation, transformational leaders need to do the following strategies:

Clearly communicate their vision: transformational leaders should be able to communicate their visions in a way that inspires employees towards achieving organization goals. This vision needs consistency as well as transparency hence creating purpose driven direction among its members.

Lead by example: transformational leaders should lead by example through practicing behaviors they expect from their teams (bass, 1985). This can only be possible when these individuals show authenticity; integrity plus strong work ethics which will motivate others emulate them too.

Empower and delegate: transformational leaders are supposed to empower employees through delegating authority including decision making processes (yukl et al., 2002). Autonomy provision coupled with sense of ownership enhances motivation levels; creativity besides commitment among other factors thereby resulting into better performance outcomes for all stakeholders involved.

Foster a culture of innovation: transformational leaders need to foster innovation within an organization where experimentation is encouraged; risks taken; continuous improvement pursued (bass & riggio). Consequently, new ideas will find space here thus stimulating innovation leading positive change.

Promote collaboration and teamwork: transformational leaders know the force that collaboration and teamwork can exert on an organization. They encourage cross-functional cooperation, maintain open communication channels, and create a supportive environment for knowledge sharing and collective problem solving.

Invest in employee development: transformational leaders understand the significance of investing in their employees' personal growth. They provide training resources such as mentorships or professional development programs that enable individuals to develop new skills and reach their full potential.

Recognize and reward achievement: transformational leaders acknowledge the contributions made by their staff members while celebrating achievements. Through recognition of exceptional performance as well as rewarding meaningful accomplishments, leaders establish a culture of excellence that encourages further growth.

Seek feedback and act on it: feedback is essential to transformational leadership because it helps leaders grow continuously. This means inviting open dialogue, listening attentively when people make suggestions or express concerns, taking necessary steps to address problems raised by subordinates.

Embrace diversity and inclusion: transformational leadership requires embracing diversity because it leads to innovation which is crucial for organizational success (sashkin & sashkin, 2003). They promote diversity in teams through recruiting people from different backgrounds so that they can have diverse perspectives thus making better decisions instead of those made by homogeneous groups (daft, 2008). It also ensures that there is fairness in terms of opportunities as well as growth and advancement among all employees without any form of discrimination.

By adopting these approaches, leaders can create a work culture founded on the principles of transformational leadership in a corporate environment. This helps to foster an empowered workforce that is both engaged and motivated to deliver its best efforts resulting in overall business growth and success.

Overcoming challenges and obstacles in implementing transformational leadership:

In corporate settings, implementing transformational leadership may face several challenges or obstacles. Understanding these barriers and having ways of overcoming them are important for maintaining positive change and maiming momentum.

One of the common challenges is resistance to change. When introducing transformative leadership practices, there might be employees who resist due to fear about what they do not understand or people who have had negative past experiences with changes in the business. In order to deal with this problem; effective communication should be emphasized whereby leaders explain the reasons behind such changes, share success stories from similar organizations and listen attentively whenever workers raise concerns. Furthermore; the involvement of staff members during the decision-making process helps them take ownership of these decisions and lead to their commitment towards their realization.

Another obstacle includes organizational inertia which refers to deeply rooted cultures preventing changes from taking place (Kotter & Cohen, 2002). This could involve middle level managers being comfortable with existing conditions hence resisting any attempts aimed at altering the status quo or even a lack of support coming from major stakeholders required for a successful implementation process. To overcome this; transformational leaders must build coalitions by seeking support from influential individuals across the whole organization (Mumford et al., 2000).

Creating a guiding coalition composed of the top management team members who are passionate about the vision statement that they have developed together is essential since such people can help in reducing resistance against new initiatives through championing 'the cause' among other subordinates as well as providing the necessary resources needed by lower rank employees during the implementation stages (bass, 1985).

Also, when implementing transformational leadership, lack of resources and time constraints can pose challenges. Organizations may face budgetary limitations or competing priorities that hinder their ability to fully invest in training programs, leadership development initiatives, or other resources necessary for transformational change. Leaders in such cases like with non-profits can explore creative solutions and leverage existing resources more effectively. They can partner with external consultants or industry experts to provide expertise and guidance. Additionally, leaders should prioritize their actions based on the impact they will have on the organization's goals and allocate resources accordingly.

Sustaining the transformational change and maintaining momentum can be a significant challenge. Over time, complacency may set in and employees may revert to old habits or resist further changes. To combat this, leaders must continually reinforce the vision and values of the transformational initiatives. Regularly communicate progress and celebrate achievements to keep employees motivated and engaged. Additionally, leaders should foster a learning culture that encourages ongoing development and improvement. By providing opportunities for continuous learning, skill-building, and personal growth, leaders can prevent stagnation and keep the momentum going.

Measuring the impact of transformational leadership in corporate organizations:

One of the key factors in assessing the effectiveness of transformational leadership in corporate settings is measuring its impact on organizational outcomes and individual growth. We delve into various methods, frameworks and tools that can be used to evaluate overall success as well as the long-term effects of transformational leadership within businesses.

1. Key performance indicators (KPIS):

To assess impact of transformational leadership, organizations can identify specific Kpis aligned with their strategic goals objectives thereby including financial metrics like revenue growth; profit margins; return on investment; non-financial measures including employee engagement rates, customer satisfaction levels, innovation adoption rates and more. These indicators are tracked over time so insights into effectiveness come from monitoring these Kpi's over different periods.

2. Employee surveys:

Employee surveys are another valuable tool for measuring the impact of transformational leadership in corporate organizations. These surveys can gauge employee perceptions of their leaders, levels of job satisfaction, commitment to the organization, and alignment with its values and vision. By collecting feedback from employees at various levels within the organization, leaders can identify areas for improvement and make data-driven decisions to enhance their transformational leadership strategies, surveys can also use Likert rating scales like the MLQ as well as provide more qualitative feedback.

3. Performance reviews and 360-degree feedback:

Performance reviews as well as 360-degree feedback processes provide a comprehensive evaluation of employees' performance including leadership capabilities; incorporating criteria related to transformational behaviors into these assessments helps organizations gather valuable insights into how effectively they foster change and inspire greatness on their teams. This feedback can inform targeted development plans for leaders and help them further enhance their transformational leadership skills.

4. Qualitative research:

Qualitative research methods offer deeper insights into the impact of transformational leadership in corporate organizations in addition to quantitative measures. Conducting interviews or focus groups with employees at different levels of the organization can provide a more nuanced understanding of the ways in which transformational leaders have influenced their work experiences, motivation, commitment etc. This qualitative data is used for identification purposes such as finding particular stories that exemplify the positive impacts done by individual teams under the guidance of their leaders.

5. Benchmarking comparisons:

Benchmarking and comparative analysis with peer companies or industry leaders can help organizations gain a broader perspective on the impact of transformational leadership. In similar contexts as highly successful transformational leaders, examining their practices and outcomes can help organizations identify areas for improvement and adopt best practices that have proven to be effective. This comparative analysis can help leaders refine their strategies and enhance their transformational leadership initiatives in a competitive field.

6. Longitudinal studies:

Conducting longitudinal studies is one way of understanding the long-term effects of transformational leadership in corporate settings. These are studies that track organizational performance and employee outcomes over an extended period thereby allowing an analysis of the sustained impact of transformational leadership initiatives. By comparing data from different time points, leaders can assess whether the positive changes resulting from transformational leadership practices endure over time and contribute to the long-term success of the organization, or fall by the wayside of a culture of indifference.

It takes a multidimensional approach involving both quantitative and qualitative measures to measure the real world impact of transformational leadership in corporate organizations. Through kpis, employee surveys, performance reviews, qualitative research, benchmarking and longitudinal studies, among other methods, leaders can fully understand how their efforts towards transformational leadership are driving positive change within their organizations and leading to lasting growth.

The present day is characterized by hyper connectivity, hence making digital transformation a necessity for all businesses. With technology advancing rapidly and customer expectations evolving while the competitive environment changes, it has become imperative for organizations to adopt digital technologies and embrace transformational leadership. However, there are difficulties associated with embarking on this transformative journey.

We will explore the challenges that businesses face in their journey towards digital transformation and offer strategies to solve them. Businesses can navigate through complexities by understanding the nuances of digital transformation and taking a proactive approach embracing the opportunities brought by the digital era.

The arduous journey of digital transformation:

Digital transformation is a process that organizations must continually adapt and change based on technological changes. Although covid-19 pandemic has been instrumental in catalyzing digital transformation efforts, firms should also recognize that this journey is iterative. This means it is not a one-time implementation but rather involves frequent learning as well as pivoting to meet new and dynamic challenges.

Participants in roundtable discussions often state how costly and time-consuming digital transformations are. As a matter of fact, 60% of companies making significant strides on their way to digital transformation take at least five years to do so. Thus, there is need for long-term planning as well as continuous technology upgrades especially focused on organizational capabilities and the talent base.

But what do we mean by digital transformation in business? Digital transformation is the integration of digital technology into all areas of business, fundamentally changing how you operate and deliver value to your clients, and employees. Not just operating a website, but implement customer relationship management, sales software, employee training programs and the day to day running of the business itself.

Guiding principles for digital transformations:

Organizations must follow certain guiding principles to overcome the challenges associated with this type of change. Such principles allow any organization regardless of its stage of development (embryonic; progressing or stalled) to have an all-round approach towards change throughout their journey. Let's discuss these guiding principles...

1. Recognize the emotional side of digital transformation:

Sometimes, going through a digital transformation process can be too much emotional burden for both employees and the leaders involved in it. The unpredictable nature of emerging digital technologies coupled with the need to create something different for customers may often lead to uncertainty amongst workers. It is important for leaders to acknowledge and respond to the emotional toll that digital transformation takes on their teams.

Leaders must embrace experimentation and the inevitable missteps and failures that come with the innovation process. Step-change innovation requires courage, and even digital-first companies struggle to make the necessary long-term investments when investors focus on short-term metrics. Creating a culture that supports psychological safety and encourages a growth mindset is essential for fostering innovation something at which transformational leaders excel.

2. Align around a customer-centric narrative:

While vision and strategy are important, they must be accompanied by shared purpose. Employees should not only know where the organization is aiming but why it is doing so as well. The relationship between an organization's identity, its clients, and how digital technology can assist in adding value need to be articulated by leaders.

A customer-centric narrative helps employees develop a shared understanding of the customer journey and the organization's purpose. It fosters collaboration, innovation, and a sense of belonging among employees. By anchoring the organization's decisions and actions to the customer's needs and desires, companies can create differentiated and meaningful experiences.

3. Build a data-informed culture by upskilling talent:

Organizations must upskill their talent to make digital tools and data work for them. Not all should be technological data wizards; however, every worker should have some basic knowledge and feel comfortable about data. Within the organization, there need to be digital specialists who can play a significant role in advancing user-friendly digital tools and promoting data literacy.

Leaders also need to note the presence of different generations, including digital natives, digital immigrants and digital refugees*, amongst their workforce. By understanding the unique perspectives and comfort levels of each group, leaders can design effective upskilling programs that cater to the needs of all employees. Reverse mentoring programs, where younger employees educate senior leaders about digital tools, can also be valuable in enhancing digital literacy.

*digital natives: people born in the digital age and comfortable with digital technologies on a daily basis from their childhood.

Digital immigrants: people who were born before the digital era and later adapted to it, often those from generation x/xennial and older.

Digital refugees: those who cannot keep up with digital technologies, find it difficult to use them and are unable to merge them into their lives.

4. Manage the power dynamics that come with data:

Data should not replace expertise or experience but it can inform and question the status quo within an organization. Leaders must manage the power dynamics that come with data and create a culture where employees would use data for better decisions which they would arrive at faster. This requires fostering psychological safety and diversity of thought within teams.

Leaders should be aware of potential biases resulting from algorithms or data-driven decision-making as well. Ensuring demographic diversity within teams and embedding ethical considerations into decision-making processes can protect against unintentional bias and build a more inclusive and ethical data culture.

5.design for inclusive and agile problem-solving:

It is important as organizations go through digital transformation that employees are empowered to own customer problems and innovate on their behalf. Leaders should design organizations that mirror the end-to-end customer experience, enabling employees to solve problems through the eyes of the customer.

Additionally, leaders must promote innovative thinking via ad-hoc problem-solving teams complimentary with the permanent organizational structures too. These teams require members with diverse skills-sets from various perspectives, hence encouraging collaboration as well as decentralization of decision making. Clarifying decision rights as well as escalation protocols is critical for ensuring efficient problem solving in this context.

6.encourage an outside-in and collaborative ecosystem perspective:

Organizations need continuous learning to achieve digital transformation and thus require outside-in perspectives. Leaders ought to arrange trips to innovation hubs and encourage interaction with people from other industries. This exposure can bring into the organization a variety of viewpoints and ideas that inspire creativity and curiosity.

Also, partnerships within different ecosystems such as private companies, government agencies, non-profit organizations are important for creating successful catalysts for change in the digital era via skill and experience transference, and a multi-perspective approach. Sometimes rivals may become partners as firms acknowledge the value of collaboration in staying cutting edge in a fast moving field. This allows organizations to take advantage of the capabilities and expertise of others, thereby promoting innovation and growth.

7.safeguard ethics and take a proactive approach to governance and compliance:

To build trust and maintain a good reputation for an organization, ethical governance of data is important. Leaders must therefore incorporate ethical judgement throughout the organization as well as plan ahead for ethical dilemmas. An "office of ethics" or ombudsman usually establishes oversight while resolving complex ethical issues, familiarity with how this system works and the rules and guidelines is a must when driving transformational change.

Organizations should also be aware of emerging compliance standards by being proactive in shaping regulations related to their activities too. By adhering to ethical principles and creating processes that reinforce desired actions, organizations can navigate ethical challenges and ensure responsible use of data and technology as well as help shape future legislative frameworks and guidelines.

Embracing the opportunities of digital transformation:

Digital transformation is a journey that necessitates commitment, agility and being 'people' focused. Acknowledging the emotional aspect of transformation, aligning to customer-centric storylines, skilling talent, managing power relationships, fostering inclusive problem-solving, embracing an ecosystem perspective and upkeeping ethics allows organizations to navigate through the challenges and take advantage of opportunities associated with future digital advances and ever-changing technologies.

To succeed in implementing digital transformation, we need empathetic transformational leaders and change catalysts who are also visionary and adaptive. They should be able to inspire their teams to work harder and better as a team. The ideal culture is about continuous learning where experimentation and innovation are the norms of the day. Organizations that embrace digital transformation can position themselves for success in an increasingly digital world.

The fast-paced and constantly changing tech industry has made transformational leadership more important than ever before. Change drivers with vision and courage, have the power to build markets and remake our world. Below we will provide inspiring examples of transformational leaders who have contributed significantly to the tech industry. These leaders have left an indelible mark on the world through their innovative mindset and ability to inspire and mobilize others to achieve transformational change.

Elon musk: revolutionizing tech world:

Elon musk is a billionaire entrepreneur and engineer who is well-known for his transformational leadership in the technology industry. His visionary approach has resulted in the formation of revolutionary firms like tesla and Spacex. He has consistently disrupted industries that were stagnant in terms of innovation.

One of his notable achievements is that he contributed to zip2's creation as well as x.com later merged with PayPal. These initiatives changed online payment systems forever and served as the foundation upon which today's e-commerce industry was laid. The pursuit of technological advancement throughout his life led him to found spacex, a company aimed at exploring space and eventually colonizing mars. Through spacex, musk hopes to realize space travel and colonization by defying human limitations.

Musk also demonstrates transformative leadership through his investment in tesla, an autonomous vehicle manufacturer that is set to disrupt the automotive sector. Musk's goal is to redesign transportation by developing electric vehicles (evs) and pioneering autonomous driving technology, thus reducing our reliance on fossil fuels. Moreover, musk's involvement with solarcity has resulted in widespread adoption of renewable energy sources hastening change within the energy industry.

Similarly, musk co-founded neuralink, which focuses on using artificial intelligence to integrate human brain technology into computers. The initiative could redefine what it means to be human in future by pushing humans' cognitive abilities beyond imagined limits through a merger with machine intelligence.

Jeff Bezos: a world market shaper:

Jeff Bezos, amazon's founder and CEO, is widely regarded as the most influential and visionary leader of the twenty-first century. His transformational leadership has played a vital role in overhauling the world business arena, changing our way of shopping as well as consumption of goods and services.

Under Bezos' stewardship, amazon evolved from being an online bookseller to a $1.7 trillion-dollar online retail behemoth. The company's strong customer focus and its push for continuous innovation have disrupted traditional retail models and set new benchmarks for e-commerce. To this end, Bezos' focus on long-term growth coupled with his readiness to take risks such as automation and 'robot' factories has always seen amazon venture into unexplored territories.

Other examples of successful enterprises besides amazon that have been built by Bezos include; blue origin which is a space exploration company and amazon web services (AWS) the leading cloud computing platform. Therefore, these ventures support the idea that Bezos is committed to driving technological advancement and exploring new frontiers.

Bezos transformed amazon into one of the most innovative firms globally through transformative leadership style. His visioning nature coupled with fearless execution of strategies has made it become a global leader in technology industry.

Reed Hastings: transforming entertainment and culture:

Launching Netflix in 1997 was a game changer for reed Hastings who became an influence in the entertainment industry, he was instrumental in enabling Netflix emerge as a dominant global platform for streaming media across internet connections.

Hastings' transformational leadership can be seen through how Netflix disrupted conventional media distribution channels. For example, Hastings changed Netflix from being a DVD rental store to a digital video service which is now enjoyed by millions globally. This move redefined the way individuals access or use entertainment outlets thus affecting their consumption patterns and how an entire industry operates.

Hastings went beyond transforming the entertainment landscape to creating a culture at work that fosters innovative management practices where employees take more responsibilities while having more freedom. This has greatly helped in attracting leading minds and provided a conducive environment for creativity and risk taking.

Jack ma: redefining e-commerce and philanthropy:

As one of the richest men in china, jack ma has immensely contributed to the tech industry through a transformative leadership approach. Alibaba is among the companies that have revolutionized e-commerce by enabling small businesses to thrive within the global digital economy shaping it significantly.

Alibaba group, which owns many different companies, has changed how people buy things in china and beyond. During his reign at Alibaba, ma developed platforms that connect buyers and sellers resulting in the success of many small enterprises during the internet era. This vision-oriented style has led Alibaba to be a global powerhouse in online commercial transactions.

Key takeaways:

In the tech industry, transformational leadership is instrumental in driving change and innovation. This has been evident in the cases of elon musk, jeff Bezos, reed Hastings, and jack ma who exemplify how visionary leadership transforms people, businesses and society.

These leaders have entirely changed industries, disrupted old models and facilitated technological advancements. They were able to motivate and mobilize others as change catalysts as well as relentlessly pursuing excellence leaving an everlasting impact on the world through their unwavering vision.

As this tech industry continues to evolve transformational leadership will remain key for driving change and defining the future.

Chapter 15

TRANSFORMATIONAL LEADERSHIP IN EDUCATION

In a digital age, transformational leadership in education is of great significance in shaping the future of our society. It becomes evident, as educational institutions face unique challenges and opportunities that transformational leadership has a significant potential to lead them towards excellence and positive change.

Within the education sector, leaders must navigate complex systems, changing policies, and diverse stakeholders while striving to create an environment that fosters optimal learning experiences for students. Transformational leaders understand the need to align their vision with their institution's objectives as well as inspire others towards a common vision of educational success.

The importance of transformational leadership in education is its ability to inspire and motivate educators, administrators, and learners to achieve their full potential. Such leaders have outstanding qualities like visionary thinking, passion, and integrity which are essential for change. By having these qualities they develop a sense of direction among followers in terms of commitment towards achieving educational greatness.

Transformational leaders in educational settings leverage their influence to create a culture of innovation, collaboration, and continuous improvement. These people encourage searching new teaching techniques; approaches in curriculum design; technology development nurturing an environment which values creativity and experimentation. Leaders motivate educators by engaging them to push beyond their 'normal' level, embracing changes and constantly improving on their teaching abilities.

One key goal of transformative leadership in education is ensuring student achievement. They recognize that every learner is different from another because everyone has his/her own gift, dreams or even learning requirements. Through a personalized approach and individualized support they ensure high student engagement promoting academic as well as personal success.

Moreover they understand the crucial role played by emotional support in creating a conducive environment for learning. Students are made to feel valued; respected or supported emotionally under this leader's culture. A sense of belongingness helps students address social-emotional issues thereby ensuring general wellness and success.

However, implementing transformational leadership within schools and colleges presents some challenges. On the one hand transformative leaders may encounter resistance from different stakeholders who are not ready to embrace change. Overcoming this resistance necessitates robust engagement skills, empathy and the capacity to articulate an incisive vision that resonates with all educational community members. In these trying times, transformational leaders will need to strike a balance between these aspects and their instinctive urge for positive change.

To sum up, the significance of transformational leadership in education can never be underestimated. It plays a critical role in guiding educational institutions towards excellence and positive change. They create a culture of innovation and collaboration by encouraging educators, administrators and students who eventually bring about student success and well-being through varied means. Even though there may be challenges in implementing transformational leadership within education systems, effective leaders tackle them with grace and determination so that their institutions continue to grow and thrive.

Transformational leaders today play a critical role in educational institutions, inspiring and motivating educators, administrators, and students to reach their full potential at all levels. These leaders possess distinct characteristics and employ specific strategies to create a transformative environment within schools and colleges.

Transformational leaders are crucial in educational settings because they provide a visionary mindset which steers the entire institution towards greatness and positive change. These individuals have a dream of where education will be in future, and are therefore able to convince others about it. For example, transformational leaders need to explain to others why they feel so passionate about their visions of how learning environments could be improved.

Moreover, transformational leaders within the field of education exhibit unwavering determination as regards their vision. They take challenges and setbacks as opportunities for development and growth. The more difficult situations they face, the stronger and more inspiring they become.

Besides empowering others, transformational leadership involves fostering trust and support within educational institutions. They believe that autonomous professionals are more effective teachers who are also happy at work. In order to build a strong team of professionals who take responsibility for their actions and contribute to student performance positively, transformational leaders train them.

Furthermore, transformational leaders understand that schools should create positive climates that emphasize emotional wellbeing and overall development. They promote personalized learning approaches that address individual's needs with ease which makes it easier for learners to get customized experiences during this process. Hence these types of school heads foster a feeling among their students that they can do great things if they put their minds on them.

Although there may be some unique challenges related to transforming leadership in education systems such as resistance or fatigue from change; nevertheless good leaders move past these hurdles smoothly. They establish strong relationships with stakeholders while involving every member of the society concerning any issue affecting them directly or indirectly on campus including reasons for positive change occurring in our institutions. Transformational leaders who listen and follow up are able to sustain and nurture change within educational institutions.

Finally, transformational leaders in educational institutions have a significant role to play in encouraging and inspiring educators, administrators, as well as students to realize their full potential. Through visionary mindset, unwavering determination, exceptional communication skills, empowerment of others and promotion of student success these leaders make education a transformative experience that motivates learners towards positive change.,institutionalizing transformational leadership in school/college calls for a strategic approach to cultivate a culture of innovation, collaboration and continuous improvement. This article provides practical suggestions on how educational leaders can effectively implement these principles:

Establishing vision: it is important for transformational leaders to come up with an appealing vision for the schools or colleges under their administrations that all the stakeholders will identify with. This way it becomes possible to motivate educators, administrators and even students to strive for excellence.

Effective communication: in order to implement the culture of transformational leadership transparent communication should be practiced throughout the institution. Goals must be clarified through clear communication by leader about what he or she wishes staff members to achieve within a given period of time so that they become part of their team's objectives and recommend ways of achieving them. Effective communication is trust building; it encourages collaboration; it empowers individuals to contribute from their unique perspectives.

Empower educators: leaders who transform empower educators by giving them the autonomy, support and opportunities for professional growth. As leaders give teachers a chance to try out new teaching techniques they also provide an enabling environment that is conducive in nuturing creativity and fostering the love of learning.

Foster collaboration: transformational leaders put an emphasis on the significance of collaboration between teachers, administrators and other staff. This facilitates collaborative problem-solving as well as innovation in education through encouraging interdisciplinary teams, nurturing shared decision-making platforms and establishing a sense of community.

Support continuous improvement: ongoing professional development for educators is prioritized by transformational leaders so as to enhance their skills and pedagogical practices. This entails investing in coaching, mentorship programs as well as availing relevant resources that aids in guiding continuous improvement in the teaching methodologies used and curriculum design.

Embrace technology: for educational purpose, transformational leaders use technology as a catalyst. They invest on infrastructure, digital materials and teacher training to achieve effective integration of technology into learning processes. It allows for personalized learning experiences, increase students' involvement and prepare them for digital age.

Celebrate achievements: acknowledging and celebrating achievements plays an important role in fostering a culture of innovation and continuous improvement. Transformational leaders recognize the efforts made by educators, administrators, even students themselves. In addition to this positive reinforcement inspires individuals hence reinforcing their commitment towards excellence while building pride within the education community.

Encourage risk-taking: educators are encouraged to experiment with innovative ideas by creating environments that make them feel safe sharing their thoughts. Through embracing failure as an opportunity for growth leaders create an environment that encourages innovation which fosters continuous learning.

Promote inclusive practices: transformational leaders put inclusivity first in schools or colleges thereby embracing diversity and creating a setting that honors all individuals contributions to such institutions. They engage in culturally responsive instructions besides advocating equitable access to education which contribute towards breaking down systemic barriers.

Monitor and evaluate progress: these leaders should always review progress in line with their vision and goals. In order to facilitate decision making and promote continuous improvement initiatives, they collect data on student outcomes, teacher performance and institutional effectiveness.

Implementation of transformational leadership in schools therefore requires commitment, persistence and flexibility. Practical strategies like these enable educational leaders to foster cultures of innovation, collaboration, and continuous improvement which are important for preparing students for success in our changing world.

To sum up, transformational education leaders struggle with resistance to change as well as the need to make this change last. An effective way of addressing this challenge may include stating clearly the reasons behind the transformation process by involving the most concerned parties while taking into account their worries through proper communication processes. Furthermore, engaging all shareholders in making decisions, supporting professional growth and highlighting successes can fuel these changes and positively affect educational institutions.

Digital literacy in schools an example of transformational leadership in action:

Leaders in education today understand that a rapid change in the world necessitates digital transformation to improve efficiency and effectiveness and enhance the overall learning experience. This has been further revealed by the global pandemic that emerged recently requiring agility in grasping digital technologies. Educational leaders and policymakers are faced with huge pressures of taking a systems approach towards digital innovation and transformation. We will outline a comprehensive plan for implementing digital literacy and transformative leadership in the field of education considering economic, political, social and technological trends that shape primary and secondary education.

Understanding digital transformation in education:

Digital transformation in education is not just about isolated technological innovations but it also calls for a perception shift to using technology as an instrument for effecting change as a whole. School system leaders as well as policy makers are required to grow beyond siloed digital initiatives toward a transformational mindset that responds effectively to current challenges. A clear definition of digital transformation for learning organizations is essential to guide strategic thinking and reflection.

Components of successful digital transformation:

To achieve successful digital transformation in education, several critical components need to be considered. These components are informed by thematic analysis of various digital transformation frameworks. Through understanding and implementing these components, educational institutions can maneuver through the complexities of digital transformation ensuring its effectiveness. The following section highlights key components required for successful digital transformation in education.

1. Leadership and vision:

Transformational leadership plays an important role as far as driving digital transformation within educational sectors is concerned. Educational leaders should develop a clear vision on what they mean by "digital literacy" that they can effectively articulate to all stakeholders. They should inspire their teams using techniques such as motivation to embrace change while fostering an innovation culture.

2. Digital strategy and planning:

For effective implementation of any given program on transforming digitally it requires a well-defined strategy which must be aligned with the overall objectives of the institution's educational objective (parker et al., 2019). A detailed plan should be developed outlining the steps, resources and timeframes required for successful transformation.

3. Infrastructure and resources:

For digital transformation to take place, strong infrastructure and enough resources are needed in supporting technology integration in schools (ager et al., 2020). Educational institutions should invest in reliable hardware, software, and networks. Teachers and staff must also be trained through various professional development programs so that they can effectively use technology.

4. Curriculum and instructional design:

Digital transformation should align with the curriculum and instructional practice. Educational institutions must redesign their curriculum to incorporate digital literacy skills. Instructional design should merge technology seamlessly promoting active learning, collaboration, critical thinking.

5. Stakeholder engagement and collaboration:

Digital transformation in education is a process that involves all individuals such as students, parents, teachers, administrators as well as policy makers among others (devlin-scherer et al., 2019). Engaging these stakeholders is imperative to ensure buy-in from them as well as their support throughout the process. Regular channels of communication should therefore be created for purposes of obtaining feedbacks as well as addressing any concerns that may arise.

6. Data management and privacy:

However, effective digital transformations require robust practices of data management focusing on privacy and security strongly (bates et al., 2019). There is need for educational organizations to devise mechanisms of carrying out data collection storage as well analysis protocols. Hence compliance with relevant data protection regulations is necessary for safeguarding student plus employee information.

7. Assessment and evaluation:

Digital transformation must be accompanied by appropriate assessment and evaluation strategies. Educational institutions need to develop ways of measuring the impact of digital initiatives on students' learning outcome. Regular evaluation and feedback loops enable continuous improvement and inform decision-making.

Guidelines for implementing the roadmap to digital literacy in education…

In this section, we will outline a roadmap for implementing digital literacy into educational institutions after discussing the essential parts of digital transformation in education. The roadmap includes:

Phase 1: assessing readiness and setting goals

Assessing the institution's current level of digital literacy is the first phase which involves identification of various gaps and areas that can be improved upon. This should consider infrastructure, resources, curriculum, instructional practices, stakeholder engagement. Goals and objectives should be clearly defined based on this assessment to guide the process of digital transformation.

Phase 2: developing a digital strategy

Educational institutions should therefore develop a comprehensive digital strategy that aligns with their education goals. The strategy is supposed to address these gaps specifically outlining how teaching, learning, or administrative activities will employ technology as well as budgetary allocations that may be required.

Phase 3: building infrastructure and capacity

Educational institutions have to invest in adequate infrastructural support as well as build capacity among teachers, staff and students for successful implementation of digital technologies. This includes procurement of hardware, software and networking solutions that meet the requirements of an institution. Furthermore, there should be training programs and workshops aimed at improving teacher-student skills.

Phase 4: integrating technology into the curriculum

The integration of technology into the school's curriculum is vital when it comes to promoting digital literacy. Revising their curriculum to include digital skills/competencies educational institutions ought to incorporate courses in line with technological knowhow. Active learning collaboration, problem solving and critical thinking are key during this integration process.

Phase 5: engaging stakeholders and fostering collaboration:

Involvement and participation of all stakeholders is important for successful digital efforts. Schools need to have platforms through which they can receive feedback, address concerns, and make them feel part of the process. Parents, industry leaders and community organizations can offer such assistance.

Phase 6: monitoring and evaluation:

Monitoring and evaluation are key in measuring the efficiency of digital transformation initiatives on an ongoing basis. Institutional mechanisms should be put in place where one can gather data about student progress, teacher performance, overall impact among others. This new way of doing things in education allows making decisions based on the most uptodate data while improving continuously.

Digital transformation is a complex process that demands careful planning, strategic leadership and collaboration in education. Through following these transformational steps to digital literacy as well as applying transformational leadership in schools we will be able to face the digital challenges of an uncertain future. Digital transformation is not just about using new technologies; it is about fostering a culture of innovation, adaptability, and lifelong learning. For this reason, educational institutions should prepare students for life after school by teaching them how to adapt to new technological changes at work.

Chapter 16

TRANSFORMATIONAL LEADERSHIP IN HEALTHCARE

Transformational leaders in the dynamic and complex healthcare environment face unique challenges. In order to make any changes that will lead to improved patient outcomes, leaders have to know what they are.

Advancements in medical technology, evolving regulations and increasing expectations from patients characterize a dynamic environment within which healthcare organizations operate. Moreover, leaders must address issues such as rising health care costs, access to care disparities and quality improvement while navigating these complexities.

One of the main dilemmas faced by healthcare leadership is how to balance patient care with financial sustainability. These transformational leaders must come up with inventive ways of improving patients' outcomes with limited resources. As they make decisions on patients' welfare they also have to consider the financial aspects of their decisions.

Healthcare leaders need to foster collaboration and effective communication among different stakeholders in order to work efficiently and protect budgets. For instance, in healthcare organizations there are medical teams composed of doctors, nurses, administrators and support staff who work together in providing comprehensive health services with a responsibility for commissioning care and managing care budgets. Transformational leaders should encourage teamwork and communication for better outcomes across all such departments.

Continuous adaptation and innovation are crucial in this profession. In fact today's healthcare organizations are exposed to new technologies, drugs, or research every day. Thus the transformational leader needs to be willing to be a true catalyst for change as well as inspire others within a highly constrained environment as no healthcare organization can keep pace with this relentless cycle, therefore effective change planning is important with reviews of medicinal efficacy carried out at a predefined schedule.

It requires challenging conventional methods and looking for new approaches that will create positive impact on both patient care quality and organization performance, but unlike in some business models in the healthcare sector, the pace of change must also be managed very carefully to avoid factors like stockpiling drugs now super-seeded with better medicines. .

Ethics is another important aspect of being a healthcare leader. Transformative leaders have to grapple with complex ethical issues relating to patient confidentiality, informed consent as well as organizational integrity in making their choices and promoting change, the welfare of all stakeholders takes a secondary position to the welfare of the patient. In making difficult choices between long-term sustainability of an organization versus individual patient's welfare transformational leaders have to maintain the highest ethical standards.

Transformational leaders have a life-long impact on the medical industry through embracing innovation, fostering collaboration and upholding ethical standards. Transformational leaders are vital to enhancing patient outcomes within healthcare institutions. With their visionary mindset, unwavering determination and exceptional skills of communication, these influential individuals have the potential of motivating health professionals for greatness, but may encounter large set in their way organizations and management structures that provide a unique, yet rewarding challenge.

With that said again, one of the main ways that transformational leaders affect patient outcomes is by establishing a patient-centered culture within healthcare organizations. Therefore, they create an environment where healthcare providers are driven to deliver top-quality care by focusing on the needs and welfare of patients. They foster empathy, compassion and commitment to enhance patient satisfaction and overall health improvement among all members of the health, administration, and support staff.

In addition to creating a patient-centered culture, transformational leaders also concentrate on enhancing healthcare delivery through innovative practices. This involves embracing new technologies, procedures or strategies aimed at improving efficiency and effectiveness of health services. This drives transformative leadership to encourage out-of-the-box thinking among health professionals whereby they can come up with innovative solutions to complex medical challenges. Innovation not only improves patient outcomes but also enhances organizational growth as well as competitiveness in today's dynamic healthcare landscape, innovative 'loaning' of the most uptodate equipment can help convince skeptical change blockers of the benefits with a data first approach. Indeed measuring the efficiency of different treatment plans/procedures is of vital importance when making the case for change.

Apart from this, transformational leaders in healthcare understand that engagement of the staff in teams and interdisciplinary collaboration are key to achieve enhanced patient outcomes. A cooperative and respectful environment establishes trust for healthcare practitioners to work together with their colleagues, share ideas and achieve common goals. By collaborating effectively and communicating efficiently transformational leaders promote interdisciplinary cooperation among different departments and specialties, thereby enhancing care coordination and improving patients' end results.

All in all, when it comes to improving patient outcomes, transformative leaders have a major impact. Their visionary leadership creates a ripple effect throughout the entire organization, leading to improved patient satisfaction, enhanced quality of care, and ultimately better health outcomes for all.

In healthcare's ever changing landscape; transformative leaders are responsible for fostering adaptability and innovation within organizations to system shocks like seasonal flu epidemics and nationwide or global crises like covid 19. They recognize that staying ahead of the curve requires embracing new technologies, practices, and approaches toward delivering high-quality patient care.

Building a culture that encourages innovation is perhaps one of the main if not most difficult tasks of transformational leaders in healthcare. Moreover, such people understand that innovation goes beyond just adopting new technologies or introducing new processes; it involves creating an atmosphere of continuous improvement and creativity within one's team members, difficult when time pressures are high such as within the uk national health service, but perhaps easier in private healthcare settings.

For innovative purposes the best transformational leaders provide resources such as time budgeting allowing for training and brainstorming sessions for teams to engage in calculated risk taking roleplays and sessions to sound out new approaches amongst their interdisciplinary teams. They recognize the importance of collaboration and interdisciplinary communication where breakthroughs often come at the intersection of different perspectives or knowledge bases and drive clinical excellence.

Moreover, these leaders create an environment where failure is seen as a learning opportunity rather than a setback. Theirs is a climate that embraces tests and errors irrespective of results, yet balanced in a safe manner via the use of new technologies such as artificial intelligence, virtual reality, clinical trials and roleplays. In such environments, employees are not afraid to voice out their opinion, try out new things or even make a mistake.

Additionally, transformational leaders in healthcare who foster innovation also guide their organizations through uncertain times and periods of change. They appreciate that the healthcare sector is characterized by constant shifts such as advancements in technology, changes in regulations and patient needs. These leaders proactively anticipate and adapt to these changes often putting themselves forward as rule setters rather than takers through participation on government boards and committees, ensuring that their organizations remain agile and responsive.

Again, they help create adaptability cultures by encouraging them to be open-minded flexible and embrace change. They ensure there is consistent communication of the vision for change making sure everyone understands why it is necessary and how it aligns with the organization's mission and values.

These leaders in healthcare also recognize the importance of continual learning and professional growth within their organizations. This is because they know that staying updated with best practices, new trends and developments in healthcare requires continuous learning. Moreover, this kind of leader makes it possible for others to attend conferences, get involved in training sessions and join expert networks and communities of practice, continuing professional development is compulsory in many medical professionals and this is fully supported by successful transformational leaders.

Creating a positive organizational culture in healthcare:

In healthcare, creating a positive organization culture is vital for the overall wellness of patients as well as employees. These types of leaders help establish such an environment where collaboration, teamwork and employee satisfaction is nurtured, errors result in retraining and changes to procedures not punishments except where professional misconduct is suspected.

For transformative leaders there has to be some level of trust established among colleagues within the organization so that collaboration can thrive. For instance, they often schedule regular team meetings such as inter-disciplinary rounds or shared decision-making forums. By involving health care professionals in decision making positions to participate and by valuing their feedback, particularly during decision making processes; these leaders instil confidence in their teams.

Another important attribute transformational leaders should posses is fostering a supportive working environment that enhance employee satisfaction. They acknowledge the physical as well as emotional toll accompanying such healthcare duties. Consequently, these types of leaders implement work-life balance initiatives, stress management resources and professional development programs in order to take care of their teams.

Transformational leaders who invest in the growth and development of their staff improve job satisfaction as well as the quality of patient care. They provide avenues for continuous learning and encourage ongoing professional development, enabling healthcare professionals to stay updated with the latest research and advancements in their fields.

Transformative leaders also focus on recognition and appreciation. They understand that if employees' hard work is acknowledged people are motivated to do more. In addition, these types of leaders hold major events marking milestones or recognizing exceptional contributors while providing regular feedback for continuous improvement. By doing this, they create an environment where employees are appreciated and thus remain motivated to offer the highest quality services to patients.

Apart from collaboration, employee satisfaction and recognition; transformational leaders address diversity, equity and inclusion related concerns within their health care organizations. They strive towards creating an inclusive culture that fully embraces the various aspects of diversity. Through promotion of diversity, this type of a leader ensures that patients receive culturally sensitive care while allowing staff members from different backgrounds to feel valued, not excluded, embracing different voices that are heard by everyone working within the organization.

To create a positive organizational culture in healthcare, one must have the following: commitment, intentionality and constant effort. Transformational leaders should act as role models of what they want to see in their teams by practicing values that they would want to instil into the workplace. Indeed through these actions, these leaders encourage others to adopt strong integrity, ethics and a patient-centered approach.

Transformational leaders who cultivate positive health care organization cultures lay the foundation for successful patient care and overall organizational performance. They appreciate that a healthy working environment is beneficial not only for workers but also directly affects patients' conditions. By unwaveringly working towards establishing a caring and collaborative culture; transformative leaders empower medical professionals to provide compassionate, quality care which improves patients and caregivers' wellbeing.

Addressing ethical considerations in healthcare leadership:

Firstly, ethical decision making is crucial to health care leadership. Guided by ethical principles such as autonomy, beneficence, non-maleficence and justice when making decisions that affect patient care and organizational practices transformational leaders are faced with different moral dilemmas such as allocation of scarce resources, balancing between patient autonomy and beneficence as well as ensuring confidentiality and privacy rights.

Additionally, transformational healthcare leaders must encourage an ethical climate within their organizations and all employees. Supportive environments are created by leaders through setting standards for behavior based on ethical guiding principles and leading by example along with continuous training keeping ethics at the forefront of all decision-making processes.

Transformational healthcare leaders also assume a key position in upholding ethical standards while promoting patient-centered care. They prioritize shared decision-making, informed consent, and respect for patient values and preferences. Therefore, through involving patients actively in their care plans and acknowledging their rights to autonomy transformational leaders can keep ethics at the heart of the organization.

Moreover, transformative leaders must address the power dynamics within a large healthcare system. They aim at giving all health care providers a voice to raise ethical concerns while promoting an open culture of communication. This proactive approach helps to recognize ethical pitfalls before they become large-scale issues that can endanger patients or affect organizational integrity.

Lastly, transformational healthcare leaders interact openly with medical ethics committees as well as legal counsels or other stakeholders in order to navigate complex ethical challenges. In addition, they work with interdisciplinary teams in the development of policies and protocols that are based on ethical guidelines and regulatory frameworks. Through such collaboration all aspects of ethical considerations are brought into play when decisions have to be made which involve staff members, patients or the entire organization.

By addressing these ethical dilemmas head-on, transformational healthcare leaders demonstrate the commitment to high moral standards even as they bring about positive change in their institutions. How such tests are navigated with transparency, empathy for patients, and patient-focus makes these individuals emerge as the rightful stewards of ethics in health institutions throughout the world.

A case study in transformational leadership in healthcare settings:

Modern times have brought forth an unprecedented burden on healthcare systems worldwide. To address these challenges, healthcare leaders are calling for a fundamental change in the way we provide and manage healthcare services. In order to support this change we will examine a case study in transformational leadership in a healthcare setting, identify what factors led to successful transformations and which can help guide our further efforts to bring about successful change.

Case study: transformational change in the UK:

The united kingdom is a compelling case study of a transformative shift within a healthcare system. In this example, the national health service (NHS) underwent major reforms aimed at improving quality as well as increasing utility with growing demand, an ageing domestic population at a time with budget constraint and human resource limitations. This resulted in a health service able to weather the dual storms of the covid 19 pandemic and virulent flu season without a significant drop in patient care.

Key factors responsible for success of this initiative include:

Strategic leadership: strong strategic leadership which championed its agenda for transformative change was readily apparent internally. Its leaders and managers showed the way, set up ambitious goals. Their insight as well as readiness to change, adopting tele-consultations, mass vaccination programmes in community centres and social hubs, adaptation of advanced data modelling, and the boosting of public-private partnerships were notable areas of success in a service that was otherwise struggling at the seams.

Patient-centred care: the NHS continued to emphasize patient-centered care throughout the crisis period and beyond. In decision-making, patients and their families were actively engaged via NHS focus groups to discuss and adopt social distancing rules introduced by the government that were originally thought to be too strict and needlessly cruel. It was through the NHS working in collaboration with patient groups and bereaved families that led to these rules being significantly changed along with the government guidance.

Although often thought of as highly resistant to change. During the pandemic transformative leaders within the NHS itself came to the fore and often helped mediate often chaotic government policy with empathy, ethics and social responsibility.

Chapter 17

TRANSFORMATIONAL LEADERSHIP IN GOVERNMENT AND PUBLIC SERVICE

Transformational leadership in government and public service plays a crucial role in driving positive change and addressing the unique challenges within these unique sectors. This chapter provides an insightful overview of the significance of transformational leadership specifically in government and public service settings.

There are particular difficulties that leaders who work for the government or public service have to face such as bureaucratic processes, complex regulatory frameworks and navigating the court of public opinion. Nonetheless, these challenges present opportunities for transformative leaders to make a lasting impact on society and the world around them, to drive change and improve lives for the better.

Adhering to transformational leadership principles will enable these leaders to motivate their teams towards excellence and lead to the achievement of common objectives. Traits such as visionary thinking, effective communication, and dedication to serving the public characterize transformational leaders in government and public service organizations, and many of the strategies previously discussed in earlier chapter can also be adapted to this setting too.

Transformational leaders play a critical role in driving positive change within government and the public sector. They implement innovative strategies to address complex issues and promote collaboration among stakeholders, often cutting through the traditional bureaucratic process by sheer power of vision and will. By doing so, they encourage their teams to think critically about societal problems with a view of coming up with innovative solutions.

Moreover, transformational leaders in government and public service understand the importance of transparency, accountability, and ethical decision-making. They recognize that building public trust is essential for effective governance and leadership. Thus, they build trust among the citizens and colleagues by being transparent with them through engagement platforms such as roundtables, committees, focus groups and social media, in modern transformational leadership these interactions are characterized by ethical behavior and integrity.

Another key aspect that defines transformational leadership in government and public service is addressing societal issues. These include pressing issues such as inequality, poverty, climate change and healthcare access among others thus affecting equity in society. They look forward to enhancing the quality of life for their people by advancing equal opportunities, better pay or whatever societal problems they identify as being pressing and of concern to the electorate as a whole, of course politics being politics true transformational leadership is rare, swamped by partisanship, party politics and a focus on the immediate rather than mid and long term.

Transformational leadership in government and public service is of paramount importance in driving truly positive, sustainable change and addressing the unique challenges within these sectors. Leaders who embrace transformational leadership principles can inspire their teams, foster innovation, build public trust, and address pressing societal issues. Through their efforts they have the potential for considerable influence upon societies resulting in a massive effect on peoples' well-being.transformational leaders crucial role in driving positive change within government and public service organizations leads to historic moments and truly monumental effects that resound and echo through time setting an example not just for good government but for humanity as well.

These kinds of leaders in government and public service are unyielding when it comes to achieving their goals. They are determined to overcome any obstacles that come their way. This forms motivation for their teams encouraging them not to give up even at the darkest hours.

Overall, transformational leaders in government and public service demonstrate a unique set of characteristics and behaviors that enable them to inspire and motivate their teams. Through visionary thinking, determination, effective communication, employee development, and stakeholder engagement, these leaders create a conducive environment for driving positive change and achieving collective goals.

Stakeholder engagement is a critical tool that has been used to achieve meaningful results and outcomes in public service and government organizations. For example, leaders may hold meetings with the representatives of various civil society groups as well as academics to know their views regarding what ought to be done.

Public trust is important and can be built through accountability. Transformational leaders in government and public service are accountable for their actions and those of their teams. They establish clear expectations, set measurable goals, and regularly evaluate performance to ensure that they are serving the best interests of the public.

Creating confidence and trust in government as well as public service organizations requires ethical decision-making. Transformational leaders place a high value on integrity, honesty, and fairness while making decisions. They stick to ethical principles; they think about wider welfare instead of personal benefits when making resolutions as well as consider what the long-term consequences of their choices will be for all people in society.

The importance of inspiring public trust and confidence through transformational leadership can be shown by looking at real-world examples of transformative leaders who have successfully cultivated trust and inspired transformational change.

Example 1: nelson Mandela:

Nelson Mandela, south Africa's ex-president, is widely considered a transformational leader who inspired trust among his people. He demonstrated transparency by addressing the nation openly about challenges experienced during the transition from apartheid to democracy through commitment to justice, reconciliation, and equality. He led by example thereby holding himself accountable, facilitated unity among diverse groups towards achieving a single south Africa. The pursuit of equality showed Mandela's ethical decision-making process which was indicated in his emphasis on embracing forgiveness, collaboration, and nonviolence.

Example 2: Jacinda Ardern:

Jacinda Ardern is often referred to as a transformational leader especially during crises with the prime minister being the head of new Zealand. She was transparent after promptly addressing the nation following terrorist attacks on Christchurch mosques in 2019 updating citizens on investigations and showing empathy towards affected communities. She took personal responsibility for enacting tighter gun control laws urgently and set up preventive measures against future extremist acts. In seeking healing within the damaged societies, ardern's ethical decision-making focused on compassion, unity as well as inclusion.

Example 3: sir Michael barber:

Former head of the UK prime minister's delivery unit: he had always been crucial to the public sector reform that was done by the then prime minister tony Blair. His approach focused on clear objectives, monitoring progress and ensuring accountability, known as "deliverology" . This saw him being able to make significant improvements towards the provision of public services such as healthcare and education.

Example 4: barrack Obama:

Former president of the united states: Barack Obama was a transformational leader because he made history by becoming the first black president in America, displayed charismatic communication, vision for change, and pushed significant policy initiatives like the affordable care act and Paris climate agreement. His emphasis on inclusivity, diversity, and focus on diplomacy and global cooperation defined his tenure. His qualities and achievements inspired individuals across America and around the globe.

These examples underline that transformational leaders may create trust and confidence by being transparent, accountable, and making ethical decisions. When leaders possess such characteristics, people can easily have faith in government and public service organizations which leads to collaboration, engagement, and collective action for the greater good.

A leader might have set up new policies aimed at narrowing income inequality through investment in education and job training programs for marginalized communities. Alternatively, another leader could have been instrumental in implementing strategies meant to mitigate climate change through encouraging sustainable practices as well as transitioning towards renewable sources of energy.

It is important to consider the effects of such initiatives on peoples' lives while emphasizing how this has made a difference. To society as a whole. Transformational leaders need to communicate not only their vision, but their success stories too, ideally supported by independent research. For instance, improving healthcare access could lead to reduced healthcare disparities, increased affordability and better health outcomes among the less privileged due to their initiative in transforming leadership, but without effective communication of any progress made towards this goal, stakeholders might waver in their commitment to the vision and progress may become stalled.

Due to the nature of politics, where a transformational leader's message is often undermined by opposition parties it is the role of a transformational leader to try and build cross party support maximizing vision buy-in and pushing for solutions that are greater than party or self.

Transformational leaders' ability to think beyond immediate concerns and focus on long-term sustainability makes them different from others. Therefore, influential transformational leaders within government and public service leave behind positive impacts that go far beyond their time in office, ensuring meaningful change for generations to come.

Chapter 18

LEADING THROUGH CRISIS: THE POWER OF INFLUENCE IN TIMES OF UNCERTAINTY

Crisis management has now become one of the most important skills for leaders and entrepreneurs in today's business environment, an environment which is moving at a faster pace than ever before. Success depends on the ability to remain ahead in uncertain times, see the opportunity in crisis and build a more innovative organization. Transformational leadership is fundamental in seeing companies through tough times as it possesses unique qualities that distinguish it from other leadership styles that become even more important during crisis situations.

Remember that transformational leadership is a leadership style that helps motivate employees to reach their full potential. It encourages growth and development within the team or organization promoting openness, innovation and creativity. Unlike transactional or autocratic leadership styles, transformational leadership builds trust and collaboration; it relies on intrinsic motives such as personal growth, meaningful work and purposeful life pursuit.

The advantages of transformational leadership in crisis management:

Transformational leaders can be very useful during a crisis. A good example is where these kind of leaders build relationships, empower their followers, encourage innovation and help their team go through difficult situations thereby becoming stronger. Some key benefits of transformational leadership in crisis include:

Improved morale and engagement:

Employees may feel overwhelmed or stressed during times of crisis affecting their performance levels adversely. This feeling is eliminated by transformational leaders through creating a sense of community and support. Leaders boost the morale among the team by keeping everyone informed of changes, opportunities for retraining, and promoting change through open lines of communication, addressing concerns, and recognizing employees' effort among other things. Recognition and appreciation are also helpful in boosting morale as well as employee engagement.

Increased creativity and innovation:

Creativity plays an essential role in solving problems during critical periods. Transformational leaders enhance creative thinking by developing an environment that supports innovative ideas leading to the rewards associated with them. They allow their team members to go beyond norms by taking risks, being creative or exploring new solutions; thus, they are not afraid to think out-of-the-box when necessary. By facilitating the provision of all necessary resources and support, leaders are able to build a problem solving culture driven by creativity and be a catalyst for change.

Greater organizational resilience:

Organizational resilience refers to being able to adapt and recover from disruptions to the business model. Transformational leaders aim at building a resilient organization by developing adaptive capabilities and encouraging a growth mindset. They embrace change, facilitate continuous learning and capitalize on new opportunities as they arise. Regardless of the situation, transformational leaders are able to overcome such challenges through promoting resilience in their organizations.

The role of visionary leadership during crisis:

Maintaining clear vision during a crisis is very important for success. In this case visionary leaders remain focused on what they want from their teams while communicating this effectively. It poses as a way of providing direction, purpose and stability amidst the chaos and confusion that may arise in a crisis situation. Visionaries also have the ability to see the big picture and be innovative about solving problems. They inspire others by showing them the future they wish to see for themselves or company stakeholders.

For example, apple's response during the Ebola outbreak of 2014 was one of visionary leadership. The firm came up with initiatives for funding, research into new treatments, and an application that would provide information about Ebola quickly in affected areas. By defining their response clearly through taking decisive actions, apple called upon others to contribute as well thus inspiring other people to join the cause.

Leaders must be open to new ideas and flexible in their thinking in order to maintain a clear vision during a crisis. They should also be willing to change direction if circumstances alter with a view to the end goal. Leaders can guide their team through difficult times by consistently communicating this vision and its significance.

Boosting confidence and morale of your team:

Motivation, morale, and a high level of confidence are vital for transformational leaders during a crisis. A team that is low on morale and confidence may easily disintegrate, making the crisis worse. There are various methods that can be used to empower teams even in times of crises:

Open communication:

Maintain an open line of communication. Progress should be reported back to all parties involved; this includes addressing any concerns raised by others. Team involvement is improved when everyone is aware of what is happening around them. In this way, confidence is built and motivation rises.

Recognition and appreciation:

Recognizing and appreciating the teamwork done by your team members is important here as well. Transformational leaders give credit where it's due, taking cognizance of the work done as well as acknowledging challenges overcome. This recognition also plays a role in lifting morale and boosting confidence among team members thus keeping them motivated at a difficult time.

Support and guidance:

There are various roles that transformational leaders play including providing support and guidance whenever it's needed. They serve as troubleshooters or mentors offering support where necessary within their teams. These actions promote quality assurance which makes employees feel safe and hence more involved which in turn enhances their motivation levels.

Positive attitude:

The morale of a whole team can be determined by the leader's attitude even when things seem hard or impossible (Deshpande & joseph 2009). By maintaining positivity, leaders role model this behavior and encourage positive thinking among their followers. It improves their team's spirits leading to higher levels of motivation, confidence and an improved quality of decision making throughout the organization.

Through using these strategies, transformational leaders can make staff enthusiastic, boost their self-assurance and create a sense of belonging when faced with crisis.

Promoting creativity in problem solving:

In a crisis, teams must be creative when it comes to problem-solving because it offers a platform for thinking outside the box and coming up with effective solutions. Through creating an enabling environment, providing the necessary resources as well as empowering workers to take risks, transformational leaders have the capability of promoting creativity in times of crisis.

Furthermore, creative problem solving streamlines the process of adaptation and change via innovative solutions that can enable organizations to emerge stronger from crisis. For instance, Netflix started the streaming service we know and love today in response to customer's demand for a less expensive alternative to DVD rental during the recession in 2008 which later became its main business model (miller 2016).

To encourage creativity within their organization, managers need to identify those factors that prevent staff members from being imaginative. These include things like; having a safe space for idea generation, encouraging collaboration and diverse perspectives and rewarding innovative ideas. By encouraging a culture of innovation, transformational leaders enable teams to find appropriate responses to challenge.

Communication facilitation during crisis:

Communication is vital during crisis. Therefore, transparent communication has to be facilitated by transformational leaders in order to keep team members informed, aligned with goals and motivated. This encompasses:

Regular updates and sharing of information:

Leaders should provide updates about what is happening and any changes that may have effects on his/her team thus keeping them informed and 'in the loop' this way rumors are avoided. Transparency and sharing of information coupled with open communication channels helps develop trust while at the same time keeping everyone on track.

Active listening and feedback:

By actively listening to their teams, engaging in two way conversations and constructive feedback, teams feel engaged with the process of change and will be more active in creative problem solving, helping steer the company through crisis. Mutual respect should be demonstrated with value placed on team members' feedback and opinions. By establishing trust in an environment where risks can be taken and safely managed transformational leaders create a powerful toolset to steer any business through crisis.

Positive reinforcement:

Transformational leaders reward and recognize employees who have performed well. They encourage individuals to perform beyond expectations and maintain a positive attitude towards those who underperform. Positive reinforcement enhances employee engagement, productivity, and overall effectiveness of the team.

Delegation:

Effective transformations leaders give tasks to the right individuals or teams who will accomplish them efficiently. They foster development of new skills in team members by assigning challenging tasks that stretch their abilities. By doing this they motivate subordinates as well as create loyalty among them and a sense of purpose reducing absenteeism and staff turnover at points of crisis, steadying the ship.

Motivation

Transformational leaders keep their team motivated through criss by using different techniques including: setting clear goals; inspiring employees through visionary leadership; giving them autonomy to carry out their duties; and creating a sense of belonging where everyone is treated fairly.

The importance of transformational leadership in crisis management cannot be overstated. In difficult times, these leaders help the team through inspiration and empowerment, clear vision, confidence building, creativity stimulation, communication facilitation, emotionally intelligent leadership and the promotion of continuous learning and skillful problem solving.

In the contemporary fast-changing business environment that is characterized by high volatility, being able to make sense out of uncertainty and come out with a more robust innovative organization is critical for success. Transformational leadership can help managers handle crises effectively, build resilience and drive organizational growth.

Chapter 19

TRANSFORMATIONAL LEADERSHIP AND DRIVING CHANGE THROUGH DIVERSITY

It is important to consider the intersection of diversity and transformational leadership, which forms the basis for building agents of change. We will focus on why diversity matters in transformational leadership and how diverse points of view, backgrounds and experiences foster innovative thinking and problem-solving within complex organizations.

Transformational leadership can significantly benefit an organization by fostering a culture of diversity. Leaders who embrace diverse cultures, demographics and backgrounds expose themselves to a range of unique perspectives that can challenge conventional views held by many people. These varied viewpoints encourage novel thoughts, stimulate creativity and open up new possibilities for solving complex problems.

Moreover, research has consistently shown that when it comes to performance, heterogeneous teams outdo homogeneous ones. When persons with different cognitive styles, knowledge bases, and problem-solving strategies come together, there is bound to be a variety in thinking as well as decision making. This implies that individuals make better decisions by considering multiple perspectives which often leads to higher rates of innovation and better outputs.

However, promoting diversity in leadership roles can be challenging due to biases and systemic barriers that exist within many complex organizations. To overcome such biases; therefore, transformational leaders should take steps towards encouraging inclusiveness at all levels. This includes providing underrepresented groups with professional development opportunities, ensuring they have access to resources on equal terms to their counterparts while also fostering an inclusive climate of respect, respect for self, religion and culture.

For transformational leaders who would like to develop inclusive leadership competencies they need to focus on effective communication skills based on empathy and cultural intelligence. They should also encourage diverse contributions during discussions where every member feels their voice counts, hence promoting a genuine understanding of the cultural dynamics prevalent among members within an organization. By doing this they will make every employee feel valued and hence perform favorably in their respective departments, fields and roles.

Thus embracing diversity as a catalyst for lasting change is necessary for transformational leaders; they should value and actively promote diversity by creating an inclusive culture that encourages collaboration as well as creativity leading to increased engagement among all employees with cultural awareness an integral part of team management. Through the implementation of diverse opinions, transformational leaders can stimulate creative thinking to find varied solutions to complex business problems.

In addition, inclusive practices establish a working environment whereby everyone feels valued and respected for their contribution. This sense of belonging enhances loyalty, motivation and devotion to business goals among members of the team, which further results in heightened productivity. When people feel safe enough to share their thoughts, they become more involved in committing themselves to the organization's goals and objectives. These various perspectives also ensure fewer blind spots and an improved possibility of identifying risks early.

Additionally, inclusive practices contribute towards employee satisfaction and retention rates. By making individuals feel valued and included, they are more likely to stay with an organization for a long time. This also helps reduce turnover costs as well as foster a feeling of continuity and stability within the organization. Moreover, organizations that prioritize inclusivity are more likely to attract top talent from diverse backgrounds thus having a stronger innovative workforce and larger talent pool.

To effectively drive transformative change within their organizations transformational leaders must be able to leverage diversity appropriately. By actively promoting inclusivity, fostering collaboration as well as valuing divergent views they will set up a culture that encourages continuous improvement, innovation and growth. It is through these inclusive approaches that transformational leaders will tap the full potential of their groups hence ensuring lasting change.

Overcoming challenges and biases in promoting diversity in leadership:

Any effort to optimize the benefits of diversity in transformational leadership calls for addressing common challenges and biases that hinder diversity in leadership positions. Although there has been some progress over the past few years, organizations still face obstacles when trying to promote diverse leaders. In order to overcome these obstacles and foster a more inclusive leadership landscape, it is important to understand and acknowledge these challenges as well as other biases such leaders may face.

One of the problems that organizations often face is the lack of diverse candidates in their talent pool. This situation has come about due to historical disparities in access to education and opportunities among certain groups as well as cultural perceptions of various roles, for example many police forces in America are seen as not representing African Americans this in turn reduces the number of African American's that want to join these police forces leading to a cycle of under representation and a lack of diversity. As such, proactive measures must be taken to ensure equal opportunities for people from underrepresented backgrounds. This can involve having targeted recruitment initiatives, partnering with various professional networks which are diverse, or even creating mentoring and development programs specific for diverse candidates.

Unconscious bias also poses a challenge because this hampers the growth of diversified leaders. Unconscious bias refers to mental shortcuts that we do automatically without our awareness based on stereotyping or preconceived notions. These biases can affect decision-making processes that may result in promoting individuals who fit traditional leadership moulds but not those who bring out different perspectives and experiences. In order to fight unconscious bias, organizations should have a diversity training program that raises consciousness as well as offers tools for minimizing biases at hiring; promotion and performance management processes.

An example of unconscious bias can be found in the automatic screening of applications for keywords many of which are more commonly used in the vernacular of people from a certain background, in order to overcome this a transformational leader might look at hiring more representative human resources personal to go through a sample of rejected applications for other roles and check that systems are not unconsciously screening out top talent from different backgrounds, this is particularly true in the age of ai were biases in training data might be reflected in bias in the screening of potential applicants.

There might also be unconscious bias in individuals who feel that meritocracy will be compromised by promoting diversity. It is necessary to address these concerns by encouraging open dialogue and providing evidence-based arguments that highlight the value of diversity in driving innovation, creativity, and business outcomes. These conversations can be guided by transformational leaders who can also create a culture of inclusion where all voices are heard and respected.

Promoting diversity in leadership requires not only long-term commitment but also a cultural shift within organizations. Transformational leaders should start by stating their commitment to diversity and inclusion at the top level and making themselves accountable for promoting diversity in leadership roles. To this end, organizations must embrace diversity metrics and goals, as well as create diverse selection committees and leadership development programs that provide opportunities for underrepresented persons to grow and thrive.

Inclusive leadership intrinsically relies on effective communication skills. Being able to communicate openly and transparently with team members is one critical skill for transformational leaders which helps ensure everyone feels heard and valued. This includes actively listening to different perspectives, encouraging open dialogue, and creating spaces for diverse voices to be heard.

Another important component of inclusive leadership is empathy. By understanding and empathizing with the thoughts, backgrounds, experiences, cultures and challenges of people from differently cultured backgrounds, transformational leaders build meaningful connections fostering an inclusive culture. When these leaders put themselves into others' shoes, it results in an environment where everyone feels valued.

Lastly, inclusive leadership requires self-reflection and continuous learning. Transformational leaders need to constantly assess their biases, assumptions as well as privileges in order not to perpetuate inequality. Leaders can enhance their inclusive leadership abilities by continuously educating themselves on these matters and obtaining feedback from other people.

Diverse perspectives are highly valued and sought after by transformational leaders through these inclusive leadership skills they cultivate. They can make possible transformative change in their organizations by building a culture of inclusivity through effective communication, empathy, cultural intelligence, creating opportunities for growth and continuous self-reflection.

For example Indra Nooyi who was a CEO at Pepsico embraced diversity by hiring employees who had different cultures in her organization. Under her stewardship Pepsico experienced rapid growth associated with its inclusive culture.

Similarly, Microsoft's CEO Satya Nadella has prioritized diversity within Microsoft corporation. He stressed the importance of developing an all-inclusive work environment where everyone feels like they belong regardless of their background. This approach helped improve Microsoft's image while contributing to its growth through constant innovation, staying on top of development in a fast-changing it industry.

"diversity is not just about differences; it's about embracing the richness of unique perspectives that weave the tapestry of innovation and progress."

Chapter 20

TRANSFORMATIONAL LEADERSHIP AND ETHICAL DECISION MAKING

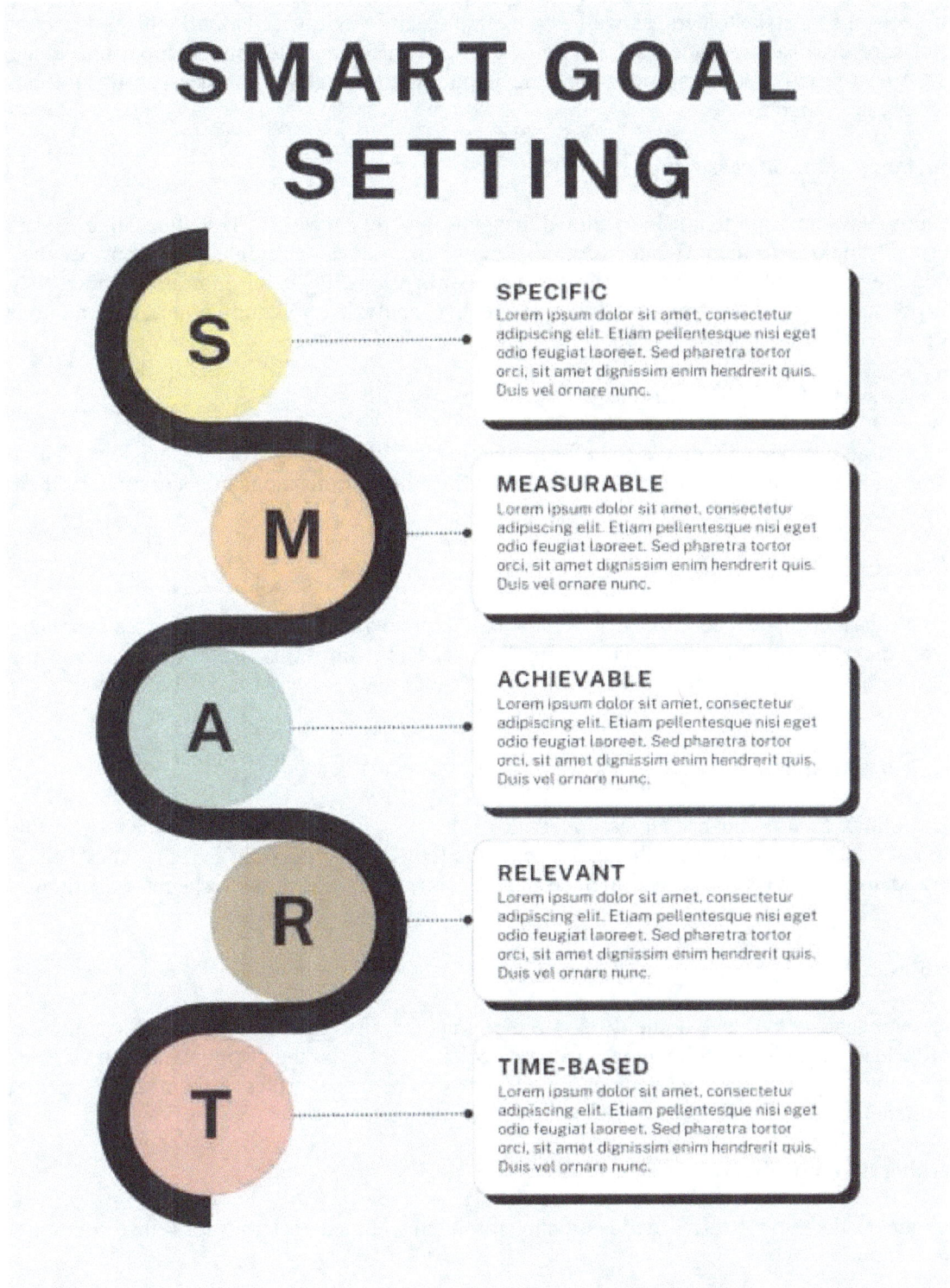

SMART GOAL SETTING

S

SPECIFIC
Lorem ipsum dolor sit amet, consectetur adipiscing elit. Etiam pellentesque nisi eget odio feugiat laoreet. Sed pharetra tortor orci, sit amet dignissim enim hendrerit quis. Duis vel ornare nunc.

M

MEASURABLE
Lorem ipsum dolor sit amet, consectetur adipiscing elit. Etiam pellentesque nisi eget odio feugiat laoreet. Sed pharetra tortor orci, sit amet dignissim enim hendrerit quis. Duis vel ornare nunc.

A

ACHIEVABLE
Lorem ipsum dolor sit amet, consectetur adipiscing elit. Etiam pellentesque nisi eget odio feugiat laoreet. Sed pharetra tortor orci, sit amet dignissim enim hendrerit quis. Duis vel ornare nunc.

R

RELEVANT
Lorem ipsum dolor sit amet, consectetur adipiscing elit. Etiam pellentesque nisi eget odio feugiat laoreet. Sed pharetra tortor orci, sit amet dignissim enim hendrerit quis. Duis vel ornare nunc.

T

TIME-BASED
Lorem ipsum dolor sit amet, consectetur adipiscing elit. Etiam pellentesque nisi eget odio feugiat laoreet. Sed pharetra tortor orci, sit amet dignissim enim hendrerit quis. Duis vel ornare nunc.

Ethical decision-making is a very important aspect of transformational leadership. In trying to create lasting change as well as inspire others, leaders have to deal with situations that are complex and demand analysis of ethical principles and values. This section examines the process of ethical decision-making for transformative leaders by providing different frameworks and approaches which enable ethical choices and acts.

1. Understanding ethical decision-making:

Ethical decision-making involves appraising possible courses of action and choosing one that is in line with moral standards and values. It necessitates being mindful of the potential consequences that may follow from decisions on stakeholders, as well as the ethical nature involved. Not all ethical decisions are straightforward because the leader is often caught up in conflicting interests or opposing values. Nevertheless, transformative leaders understand the importance of making choices based on ethics which put the greatest good first.

2. The importance of moral reasoning:

Moral reasoning plays an important role in ethical decision-making processes. Transformative leaders engage in critical thinking to identify and weigh different ethical considerations. They consider their actions within the context of principles, values, or moral obligations. By using moral reasoning, they can examine potential alternatives from an ethical perspective, analyzing how individuals, communities or organizations will be affected by their choices.

3. Ethical frameworks for decision-making:

Several ethical frameworks can guide transformative leaders in making sound decisions. These frameworks provide a structured approach to considering the ethical dimensions of a situation and help leaders navigate complex dilemmas.

A) utilitarianism:

According to utilitarianism, decisions made should be based on how much happiness they can create or maximize for most people involved. Transformative leaders using this framework assess the consequences of their actions and aim to select the option that yields the most favorable outcomes for stakeholders.

B) deontological ethics:

Deontological ethics focuses on principles and duties rather than outcomes. Leaders who use this approach do not care about what might happen to them as long as they do what is right. They follow ethical rules and take decisions based on principles such as honesty, fairness, and respect for the dignity of others.

C) virtue ethics:

Virtue ethics emphasizes the development of virtue character traits and personal moral excellence. Transformative leaders using this framework evaluate decisions based on their alignment with virtuous values, such as integrity, courage, and compassion. They try to be these virtues in their actions so that others can imitate them.

4. Ethical leadership models:

Transformational leadership models provide guidance for making ethical decisions for transformational leaders. For example:

    A. The four-component model of ethical leadership has been developed to include moral personhood, ethical influence processes, moral reasoning, and ethical behavior.

B. Integrative ethical leadership model emphasizes combining ethical decision-making with other leadership practices like promoting a culture of ethics in organizations, instilling an ethical accountability as well as advancing social responsibility.

By understanding these frameworks and models well transformative leaders are able to approach their ethical decision-making process with clarity and intentionality. They can look at options from different angles, evaluate how each choice will affect them in future and work towards being consistent in what they do based on their values and principles of ethics.

Ethical decision making is an integral part of transformational leadership. By engaging in moral reasoning and utilizing the various frameworks and models, leaders can approach complex situations with a strong ethical foundation. Therefore, transformative leaders can face the challenges that come their way while remaining committed to their aim of positive change by carefully considering how their decisions could affect all parties involved and acting on them upon principle.

Moral values are crucial in transformational leadership. As a result, transformative leaders use these values to guide their actions, make decisions, and interact with others. Transformative leaders who live by their core principles inspire trust, loyalty, and a sense of authenticity among their followers.

Moreover, moral values serve as guiding principles for transformative leaders when making tough choices. They base their decisions on their core values when faced with complex challenges or ethical dilemmas. These types of decision-makers' analyses always go beyond immediate consequences because they consider individuals involved thereof as well as the long-term implications for the organization as a whole.

One of the most common ethical dilemmas that transformative leaders face is the balance between organizational goals and personal welfare. On numerous occasions, leaders are assigned to drive organizational success by attaining certain targets or objectives. However, there are times in which they may find themselves compromising some individual's interests within the organization while pursuing these objectives. The balancing act between the needs of an organization and those of individuals necessitates careful deliberation and ethical judgement. Key to this process is the maintenance of impartiality and fairness in decision-making processes.

Some strategies for dealing with these ethical challenges include:

1. Reflecting on personal values: transformative leaders should reflect upon their core values frequently so as to make sure that they conduct themselves along these lines. This self-awareness serves as a compass for ethical decision-making.
2. Seeking diverse perspectives: another way through which leaders could address moral issues involves taking into consideration opinions from different angles hence enlightening them before making any resolution about a problem they face regarding morality leading therefore to inclusiveness without bias.
3. Engaging in ethical dialogue: open dialogue among employees fosters an environment that clearly communicates expectations in terms of ethical behaviors. Encouraging team members to voice concerns and contribute to ethical decision-making enhances trust and collective ownership.
4. Consulting ethical frameworks: transformative leaders can use established ethical frameworks to navigate through complex dilemmas. Ethical models such as utilitarian approach, deontological ethics and virtue ethics help address ethical challenges using structured processes.
5. Prioritizing long-term impact: transformational leaders should keep their focus on the long-term impact of their actions and avoid succumbing to short-term pressures. This requires maintaining a clear vision and staying committed to sustainable growth and positive change.
6. Setting ethical standards: clearly defining and communicating ethical expectations within the organization establishes a strong foundation for decision-making. This includes establishing a code of conduct and implementing mechanisms for accountability.

Transformative leaders who are intentional about examining the moral dimensions of their leadership can handle ethical and moral dilemmas with integrity ensuring that they bring about positive change while still upholding their own morals. Ultimately, by addressing ethical challenges head-on, transformational leaders can inspire trust, loyalty, and genuine transformation within their organizations and communities.

"our ethics is the compass that guides us through the moral maze, reminding us that the true measure of success is not just what we achieve, but how we achieve it."

Chapter 21

CHALLENGES AND LIMITATIONS IN MEASURING TRANSFORMATIONAL LEADERSHIP

Evaluating how far transformational leadership goes is very complicated as it necessitates looking at both intangible and tangible factors. Assessing the success and long-term impacts of transformational leadership is fraught with various problems and limitations that must be dealt with prudently to ensure the accuracy of evaluation.

One of the major challenges includes potential bias in evaluating the impact of transformational leadership. When assessing the results, evaluators may have predispositions or preferences that can influence their judgement leading to subjective understanding of the results. This challenge can be addressed by setting up a uniform criterion that is objective or nonpartisan for evaluation. A multi-rater source is also useful as it minimizes individual biases and provides more comprehensive perspectives about the impact of transformational leadership.

Additionally, quantifying intangible outcomes poses another challenge in determining the impact of transformational leadership. Usually, there are transformative corporate cultures, improved staff participation levels, and innovativeness under a transformational leader which are difficult to measure numerically. Such invisible consequences include increased employee morale, enhanced creativity among employees and other factors showing that team members are getting a meaning from what they do together. These concealed effects while being essential for overall performance of an organization are not easily measured quantitatively using traditional methods. To overcome this obstacle, a mixed method approach should be used which combines both quantitative measures (e.g. Surveys, metrics) and qualitative data (e.g., interviews and focus groups), so that all possible types of impacts could be captured.

In addition, one should consider that transformation takes time to manifest fully hence the effects of any given action or leadership objective may not appear immediately or even be measurable at times. Evaluations over long periods have to be conducted so as to determine the long lasting effect on organizations. Hence longitudinal studies ought to be conducted spanning a considerable time frame to enable evaluators to comprehend the enduring influence of transformational leadership.

Further, contextual factors should be taken into account, as these may affect how the impact is evaluated. There exist unique complexities and dynamics in different organizations and industries which can impact on the outcomes and interpretation of a transformational leadership impact. The assessors need to take into consideration such factors when designing evaluation frameworks as well as interpreting their findings for them to be relevant with respect to sometimes quite specific organizational circumstances as well as provide a holistic understanding of the impact of transformational leadership itself.

To make an impact evaluation more accurate, evaluators might use multiple data sources and triangulation techniques. Collecting information from different stakeholders including employees, customers, and performance metrics of an organization helps draw a more holistic picture.

Final thoughts:

In "the power of influence: cultivating catalysts, unveiling the forces behind transformational leadership" we have explored the intricate world of leadership and the power of influence in driving lasting change. Throughout the book, we have delved into the concept of catalysts and their role in igniting transformational leadership in a variety of settings including practical strategies to drive and promote change, overcome barriers to change and ultimately become a transformational leader and catalyst for change.

We have learned that catalysts possess key characteristics such as a visionary mindset, unwavering determination, and exceptional communication skills. These traits enable them to create an environment that fosters innovation, creativity, and collaboration among their followers.

Furthermore, we have examined various leadership theories and models, including charismatic leadership, servant leadership, transactional leadership, authentic leadership, and their relationships with transformational leadership. Each approach brings unique qualities to inspire greatness and generate positive change.

As we reflect on our personal growth as transformative leaders, it is important to consider how we can cultivate catalysts within ourselves and others. By developing personal influence, overcoming challenges, and creating a positive impact within our organizations and communities, we can effectively drive transformational change.

To cultivate catalysts, we can employ practical strategies such as enhancing credibility, building trust, gaining respect from followers, empowering others through mentorship and coaching, using effective communication techniques like storytelling and active listening, leading with emotional intelligence, understanding the ethical dimension of leadership, and continuously evaluating the impact of our efforts.

Let us remember the transformative power of influence in leadership. By applying the knowledge gained from this book, we have the opportunity to become catalysts for lasting change. Let us embrace our role in cultivating catalysts within ourselves and inspiring others to join us on this journey. Together, we can make a meaningful difference and create a positive impact that lasts far beyond our time.

Finally, we urge you to apply the knowledge gained from this book in your leadership roles, communities, or organizations. Be a catalyst for lasting change by embracing your true leadership potential. As you embark on this journey, remember that every small action has the potential to create a ripple effect that leads to meaningful impact. You have the power to inspire others and make a positive difference in the world.

Cultivate the catalysts within yourself and others, harness the power of influence, and be the transformational leader that drives lasting change. The world needs your unique abilities and perspective. Embrace this calling, and together, let's create a future filled with inspiration, innovation, and transformation.

Thank you for joining us on this enlightening journey into the power of influence and transformational leadership. May you continue to strive for greatness as a catalyst for lasting change.

"leadership is not just about navigating the present; it's about igniting the flames of change. A true leader serves as a catalyst, turning challenges into opportunities and inspiring others to embrace the winds of transformation. In the dance of progress, transformational leaders don't just follow the rhythm; they create it, becoming the catalysts that propel change and shape a brighter future."

"go forth and conquer

For the world is small

And you are the giant

And in every step

You take will make the ground shake

As it rises

To meet you."

— from Atticus poetry, 'love her wild'.

Bibliography and references:

Bass, b. M., & r. E. Riggio. 2006. Transformational leadership (2nd ed.). Mahwah, nj: Lawrence Erlbaum associates.

Kaufman, s. B., j. C. Kaufman, and p. Kaufman. 2015. "applying the genius s.a.g.e. Model to the development of catalyst skills." Journal of intelligence 3(2): 81-100.

Agarwal, u. A., Datta, s., Blake-beard, s., & Bhargava, s. (2012). Linking lmx, inclusive leadership and workplace diversity to employee satisfaction and commitment. Revista de psicología del trabajo y de las organizations, 28(1), 45-3.

Bass, b. M., & riggio, r. E. (2006). Transformational leadership. Psychology press.

Bennis, w. (2009). On becoming a leader. New york, ny: basic books.

Blake-beard, s., o'neill, r. M., & mcgowan, e. M. (2007). Blind dates? The importance of matching writing experiences to formations of multiple identities in the workplace. Management communication quarterly, 21(1), 17-33.

Finkelstein, s. (2003). Why smart executives fail and what you can learn from their mistakes. New york: portfolio.

Hamel, g. (2012). What matters now: how to win in a world of relentless change, ferocious competition, and unstoppable innovation. John wiley & sons.

Hill, l.a. & jones, g.r. (2010). Essentials of strategic management. Hampshire: cengage learning business press.

Ibarra, h. (2015). Act like a leader, think like a leader. Harvard business review press.

Kolditz, t. (2007). In extremis leadership: leading as if your life depended on it. John wiley & sons.

Kotter, j. P. (2014). Accelerate: building strategic agility for a faster-moving world. Harvard business review press.

Lombardo, m. M., & eichinger, r. W. (2000). High potentials as high learners. Human resource management, 39(4), 321-329.

Lombardo, m., ruderman, m. And mccauley c. (1988), "excellence in selection" in exercises in leadership, center for creative leadership: greensboro, nc.

Tuckman, b. W. (1965). Developmental sequence in small groups. Psychological bulletin, 63(6), 384.

Waters, j. A., & marzano, r. J. (2006). School district leadership that works: the effect of superintendent leadership on student achievement. Ers spectrum, 25(2), 1-12.

Zaff, j. F., & hair, e. C. (2003). Positive development of the self: self-concept, self-esteem, and identity. Handbook of positive psychology, 272-284.

Avci, a. (2015). Investigation of transformational and transactional leadership styles of school principals, and evaluation of them in terms of educational administration. Educational research and reviews, 10(20), 2758-2767.

Bass, b. M., & riggio, r. E. (2006). Transformational leadership. Psychology press.

Leith wood, k., & jantzi, d. (1999). Transformational school leadership effects: a replication. School effectiveness and school improvement, 10(4), 451-479.

Leith wood, k., & jantzi, d. (2006). Transformational school leadership for large-scale reform: effects on students, teachers, and their classroom practices. School effectiveness and school improvement, 17(2), 201-227.

Mascall, b., Leith wood, k., straus, t., & sacks, r. (2008). The relationship between distributed leadership and teachers' academic optimism. Journal of educational administration, 46(2), 214-228.

Printy, s. M. (2010). Principals' influence on instructional quality: insights from us schools. School leadership and management, 30(2), 111-126.

Robinson, v., lloyd, c., & rowe, k. (2008). The impact of leadership on student outcomes: an analysis of the differential effects of leadership types. Educational administration quarterly, 44(5), 635-674.

Sergiovanni, t. J. (2007). Rethinking leadership: a collection of articles. Corwin press.

Somech, a., & drach-zahavy, a. (2013). Translating team creativity to innovation implementation: the role of team composition and climate for innovation. Journal of management, 39(3), 684-708.

Hallinger, p. (2003). Leading educational change: reflections on the practice of instructional and transformational leadership. Cambridge journal of education, 33(3), 329-352.

Hallinger, p., & heck, r. H. (2010). Collaborative leadership and school improvement: understanding the impact on school capacity and student learning. School leadership and management, 30(2), 95-110.

Somech, a. (2005). Teachers' personal and team empowerment and their relations to organizational outcomes: contradictory or compatible constructs? Educational administration quarterly, 41(2), 237-266.

Hellinger, p., & Leith wood, k. (1998). Unseen forces: the impact of social culture on school leadership. Peabody journal of education, 73(2), 126-151.

Avolio, b. J., & Gardner, w. L. (2005). Authentic leadership development: getting to the root of positive forms of leadership. The leadership quarterly, 16(3), 315-338.

Avolio, b. J., walumbwa, f. O., & weber, t. J. (2009). Leadership: current theories, research, and future directions. Annual review of psychology, 60, 421-449.

Bass, b. M. (1985). Leadership and performance beyond expectations. Collier macmillan.

Bass, b. M. (1999). Two decades of research and development in transformational leadership. European journal of work and organizational psychology, 8(1), 9-32.

Bass, b. M., & Avolio, b. J. (1994). Improving organizational effectiveness through transformational leadership. Sage.

Bass, b. M., & Riggio, r. E. (2006). Transformational leadership. Psychology press.

Daft, r. L. (2008). The leadership experience. Cengage learning.

Deshpandé, r., & joseph, j. (2009). The impact of transformational leadership on business-unit innovation: moderating role of environmental dynamism and complexity. Journal of applied psychology, 94(4), 887.

Goffee, r., & jones, g. (2013). Creating the best workplace on earth. Harvard business review, 91(5), 98-106.

Griffin, g. (2008). Your leadership style: transformational? Transactional? Autocratic? A case example for nursing. Medsurg nursing, 17(1), 23.

Judge, t. A., & piccolo, r. F. (2004). Transformational and transactional leadership: a meta-analytic test of their relative validity. Journal of applied psychology, 89(5), 755.

Kellerman, b. (2004). Bad leadership: what it is, how it happens, why it matters. Harvard business press.

Lian, h., & tui, l. P. (2012). Leadership styles and organizational citizenship behavior: the mediating effect of subordinates' competence and downward trust. The journal of applied business and economics, 13(1), 59.

Miller, d. (2016). Netflix: the secret sauce for a culture of innovation. Business horizons, 59(4), 375-385.

Mumford, m. D., scott, g. M., gaddis, b., & strange, j. M. (2002). Leading creative people: orchestrating expertise and relationships. The leadership quarterly, 13(6), 705-750.

Northouse, p. G. (2018). Leadership: theory and practice. Sage publications.

Olguin, d. J. (2013). An ethnographic study of employee engagement in the workplace. (doctoral dissertation, iowa state university).

Parker, p., hall, d. T., & kram, k. E. (2008). Peer coaching: a relational process for accelerating career learning. Academy of management learning & education, 7(4), 487-503.

Sashkin, m., & sashkin, m. G. (2003). Leadership that matters. Berrett-koehler publishers.

Schein, e. (1992). Organizational culture and leadership (vol. 2). San Francisco: Jossey-bass.

www.ingramcontent.com/pod-product-compliance
Lightning Source LLC
Chambersburg PA
CBHW080850120626
46546CB00008B/2771